T0358253

Cambridge Elements ☰

Elements in Historical Theory and Practice
edited by
Daniel Woolf
Queen's University, Ontario

CONCEPTUALIZING THE HISTORY OF THE PRESENT TIME

María Inés Mudrovcic
National University of Comahue
IPEHCS-Patagonian Institute of Studies on
Humanities and Social Sciences

CAMBRIDGE
UNIVERSITY PRESS

Shaftesbury Road, Cambridge CB2 8EA, United Kingdom

One Liberty Plaza, 20th Floor, New York, NY 10006, USA

477 Williamstown Road, Port Melbourne, VIC 3207, Australia

314–321, 3rd Floor, Plot 3, Splendor Forum, Jasola District Centre, New Delhi – 110025, India

103 Penang Road, #05–06/07, Visioncrest Commercial, Singapore 238467

Cambridge University Press is part of Cambridge University Press & Assessment, a department of the University of Cambridge

We share the University's mission to contribute to society through the pursuit of education, learning and research at the highest international levels of excellence.

www.cambridge.org
Information on this title: www.cambridge.org/9781009517836

DOI: 10.1017/9781009047739

First published 2024

A catalogue record for this publication is available from the British Library.

ISBN 978-1-009-51783-6 Hardback
ISBN 978-1-009-04855-2 Paperback
ISSN 2634-8616 (online)
ISSN 2634-8608 (print)

Conceptualizing the History of the Present Time

Elements in Historical Theory and Practice

DOI: 10.1017/9781009047739
First published online: May 2024

María Inés Mudrovcic
National University of Comahue IPEHCS-Patagonian Institute of Studies on Humanities and Social Sciences

Author for correspondence: María Inés Mudrovcic, mmudrovcic@gmail.com

Abstract: In this work, we explore four meanings of the concept of contemporary, emphasizing its designation as a historical field. We argue that disagreements about when the present or the contemporary era begins stem from historians assuming a linear, chronological and absolute conception of time. Following scholars like L. Descombes, L. Hölscher, B. Latour, D. J. Wilcox and S. Tanaka, we propose conceiving relational historical time without chronology, highlighting the original sense of sharing the same time that the term "contemporary" acquired for the first time. This perspective mitigates issues concerning the beginnings or the meaning of the present. Accentuating relationships within a relational time framework aids in overcoming ontological challenges like too many presents or distance in time, along with the corresponding epistemological issue of objectivity. This Element aims to reevaluate and enrich our understanding of the multifaceted concept of the present in the context of history.

Keywords: present time, history, memory, current times, historical temporality

ISBNs: 9781009517836 (HB), 9781009048552 (PB), 9781009047739 (OC)
ISSNs: 2634-8616 (online), 2634-8608 (print)

Contents

1 The Present, the Contemporary and the Order of Time

1.1 Introduction

What does it mean to be contemporary? This question first appeared in France in the nineteenth century, and it is still asked today. It appears not only in historical reflections but also in the disciplines of literature, literary criticism (Agamben 2009; Esthel 2013; Groom 2013), anthropology (Fabian 1983) and philosophy (Barthes 2009, p. 50; Gadamer 1989), among others. Aware of this great ambiguity, Joel Burges and Amy Elias (2016) in a recent book cease using the word "contemporary" to describe the present. Even when their central objective is to build a "vocabulary of the present," they avoid engaging in "debates on how to define 'the contemporary' as a 'period maker'" (p. 2). However, despite these precautions, in their introduction, they equate the present with the contemporary and deem the postwar period our present. They understand 1945 "to be a date of significant social, economic, and political change" (p. 2).

Authors as different as Geoffrey Barraclough (1964), Peter Catterall (1997), Henry Rousso (2000, pp. 230–245) and Julio Aróstegui Sánchez (2006) agree on this topic, pointing to the diversity of dates that have been considered the beginning of the contemporary. The events some historians have chosen often differ by many years, sometimes by as much as fifty years, and thus "deeply modify the meaning of the concept of 'contemporary'" (Rousso 2012, p. 231). For example, 1789 has been recognized, not only in France, but also in most European and Latin American countries, as the beginning of the contemporary epoch, an era fundamentally marked by the French Revolution. Thus Dipesh Chakrabarty (2015) points out that "the French Revolution was perhaps the first event that found expression in forms of 'epochal consciousness.'"

Most English-speaking historians do not agree with the use of this earlier date and have pointed to 1945 as the beginning of the contemporary era, especially since the Centre for Contemporary British History was founded in 1986. This center marked the end of the Second World War as the start date for its field of research (Catterall 1997, p. 441; Rousso 2012, p. 234). At that time in Great Britain, university courses "on contemporary history … appeared … with starting dates between 1880s and 1945" (Catterall 1997, p. 441). In Germany, the year 1917 or rather "the sequence 1917–1918" is used as the edge of the contemporary world, a use that began when the Institut für Zeitgeschichte (German Institute of Contemporary History) was created in 1952. This institute grew out of the Deutsches Institut für Geschichte der nationalsozialistischen Zeit (German Institute of the History of the National Socialist Era), founded in 1949. Although the institute was "concerned primarily with national socialism, the origins of the national socialist movement under the Weimar Republic" (Caterall 1997, p. 442), for Henry Rousso (2012, p. 233), it was the emergence of the first form of globalizing the contemporary as it also included the Russian Revolution, the entry of the United States into the Second World War and the end of that war in Europe. The beginning of the First World War in 1914, the year 1940 (marking the defeat of France), and the 1912–13 Balkan Wars have also been proposed as the start of the contemporary era on different occasions. Geoffrey Barraclough (1964), in his classic book *An Introduction to Contemporary History*, proposes "the years between 1890, when Bismarck withdrew from the political scene, and 1961, when Kennedy took up office as President of the United States" (p. 10).

This disparity in the dates historians have proposed is remarkable (the same situation especially occurs in the fields of philosophy and literature). How can it be, to take just one example, that Barraclough considers the French Revolution as belonging to the modern period, in contrast to a European tradition that considers this event the inauguration of the contemporary one? Can events such as the fall of the Berlin Wall or the September 11th attacks (Readman 2011) constitute new edges for the beginning of a new contemporary era? Can we suggest, like Rousso (2012), that the present of all contemporary history "begins with 'the date of the last catastrophe,'" given that most of the proposed dates align with the resolution of wars or revolutions?

If we review all the ongoing discussion that began in the nineteenth century about what should be understood as contemporary, we can distinguish at least four different meanings. (1) It indicates a temporal relationship of contemporaneity. (2) It names the nineteenth-century epochal experience of the present. (3) It designates the present for some historians of the twentieth century. (4) It designates a field of history. In what follows, I will attempt to develop these meanings of the term "contemporary" with special emphasis on the fourth item. I will argue that the disagreement about when the present or the contemporary era began occurs because historians assume a linear, chronological and absolute conception of time. Finally, following L. Descombes, L. Hölscher, B. Latour, D. J. Wilcox and S. Tanaka, I will claim that if we conceive an historical time without chronology, which was the very sense of sharing the same time that the term contemporary acquired for the first time, the majority of problems regarding the beginnings or the meaning of the present disappear. Emphasizing the relationships between activities and thinking in terms of relational time will help us in overcoming ontological problems like too many presents or distance in time, as well as its epistemological problem of objectivity as its counterpart.

2 Present As "Sharing the Same Time"

The Latin *contemporaneus* (contemporary) came from *cum* and *tempus* and first meant *sharing* the same time. Contemporary is thus an adjective that relates events that occur and people who exist at the same time, and this use of the term first appeared in France in 1475 (Rousso 2012, p. 29). Accordingly, contemporary is not synonymous with coetaneous – that is, it does not allude merely to the temporal synchronization of "*living* at the same time." According to Vincent Descombes, "chronology defines only an indifferent contemporaneity." This is chronological contemporaneity, as Roland Barthes states in his course notes at the Collège de France:

> I can say without lying that Marx, Mallarmé, Nietzsche and Freud lived twenty-seven years together. They could even have met in a Swiss city in 1876, for example, and they could have – as "living-together" – "discussing together." Freud was then twenty years old, Nietzsche thirty-two, Mallarmé thirty-four, and Marx fifty-six. (One could ask today who is older.) This fantasy of concomitance wants to alert us to a complex phenomenon, in my opinion: contemporaneity. Whose contemporary am I? Who do I live with? The calendar does not respond well. It is what our little chronological game indicates – unless they become contemporaries now? . . . It will perhaps lead to this paradox: an unsuspected relationship between the contemporary and the untimely "like the meeting of Marx and Mallarmé, of Mallarmé and Freud at the table of time." (Barthes 2003, p. 48)

British playwright Tom Stoppard explored this sort of chronological contemporaneity in his 1974 play *Travesties*, wherein a fictional meeting between Lenin, James Joyce and Tristan Tzara occurs. Understood in this chronological way, the word "contemporary" is neither a synonymous nor an exclusive adjective of the present since it can also refer to the past and the future. Thus we can say that one of the inhabitants of Patagonia during the seventeenth century was contemporary with the English Revolution or that the future children of John and Mary will be contemporary. These examples assume a universal simultaneous chronological temporality and do not express the original meaning of sharing the same time.

An early example of the usage of this original meaning of the term "contemporary" is in the *Pensées* of Blaise Pascal, written in 1657 and published posthumously. Referring to the book Moses bequeathed to the Jews, Pascal establishes the epistemological principle that one should distrust any history not written by those who were contemporaries of the narrated events: "Any story that is not contemporary is suspect, like the books of the Sibyls, of Trismegistus, and many others that have been accepted in the world, until time has made their falsity clear. But the same does not happen with contemporary authors" (Pascal 1963, p. 436). Who considered themselves contemporaries during Pascal's time? As Hölscher points out, during the late Middle Ages, people who had not participated in a specific relationship could not have, even in their own present, a sense of having lived contemporarily or sharing the same time. During that period in European history, Pascal's era "contemporaneity presuppose[d] the mental representation of a period in which human beings live and act together" (Hölscher 2014, p. 19). That is, being contemporary, in the original sense of the term, is possible only "when humans share something, where they have a common destiny ... in which a common temporal horizon is shared" (p. 19). In Pascal's time, people lived in scattered settlements separated by long distances and lacked very fluid communication. Pascal's contemporaneity, his living or sharing in the same time, is far from the simple universal chronological simultaneity referred to in Barthes's examples. Although Mallarmé and Freud were contemporaries according to a universal chronology in the late nineteenth century, they did not live together according to Pascal's understanding of the contemporary.

In a book published just when historians and philosophers began to question historical time (Bevernage 2012; Bevernage and Lorenz 2013; Hartog 2015; Hölscher 1999; Landwehr 2014; Le Goff 1992; Lorenz 2010; Schiffman 2011), Hölscher points out that the idea of the future as we know it is relatively recent. It arose during the sixteenth and seventeenth centuries in Western Europe, and it is closely related to a new concept of history that "for the first time, conceived of the historical future as a coherent process of the evolution of humanity" (Hölscher 2014, p. 10; translation is mine). For Lucian Hölscher (2014), the salient novelty is that an idea of the future is presented as space-time, as "a period in which things have to happen, or in which they are represented as such" (p. 17). During the Middle Ages, *futurum* was a thing or an event, never the space of time. Hence the plural form *futura* was used and it makes sense to refer to singular future events. The modern concept of the future refers to a single time period or space, which does not allow the formation of a plurality: "Whenever the future is spoken of in medieval texts, it refers to 'future events,' never to the time horizon, to the period of the future as such" (p. 18; translation is mine). Similarly, the events that have occurred previously did not exist in the past – that is, a past time period they shared, but only in the memory of those who experienced and transmitted them.

> "People who have not lived in a specific social relationship cannot have, not even in their own present, the feeling of having lived 'contemporarily' ... they did not have the sensation of living in the same space or at the same time as other congeners who lived beyond the horizon of their experience" (p. 19).

Having shared common activities – that is, having lived a present – also provided them with common pasts and common futures (plural). Descombes expresses the same understanding: being contemporary is not something that can be determined by mere chronology but the common present. Those who carried out activities at the same time were contemporary because their activities were contemporary. Contemporaneity was conceived as simultaneity, a temporal relationship between activities that were carried out (Descombes 1999, pp. 29–31). In the Middle Ages, only those who had concrete social relationships could share a common experience of time; however, they had no concept of the future or the past as a uniform time. "The mental representation of a homogeneous space of time in which those future things could be related to each other" was completely unknown (p. 33). The idea of an open future and a closed past was alien to premodern Europeans. The first sense of contemporary – *cum tempus* – referred to those who share a present as the result of the interplay of activities that, because they occur simultaneously, either contradict or reinforce each other.

3 Contemporary As an Epoch

3.1 Contemporary As an Epochal Experience of Time

During the last third of the eighteenth century and throughout the nineteenth century, first in Germany and then in France and the rest of continental Europe, the adjective "contemporary" began to designate another quality of the present: an epochal experience of time. The original meaning of the Latin term *cum tempus* changed. It began to designate a distinctive characteristic of the present for those human beings who inhabited Europe after the French Revolution: "The degree to which it was understood in an epochal sense shortly after its introduction is shown by the charge leveled at Heeren that he had not explicitly begun *neueste Zeit* with the French Revolution" (Koselleck 2004, p. 244). Those who had left the feudal past shared the present or lived together. Even though Europeans maintained commercial relationships and other activities with the inhabitants of the colonies, for example, they did not consider them to belong to the same present. The contemporary present was no longer the result of common activities but a quality acquired by those who felt they were living in a new present because they had surpassed the feudal past.

The word "contemporary" is now used to identify an era or an epoch. The notion of an epoch relates to "historical consciousness" (Koselleck 2004, p. 234) or the "experience of time" (Hartog 2003, pp. 91–93) – that is, to the understanding a certain culture has of its own experience of time, which in turn informs how that culture links the present, past and future. Taine, in nineteenth-century France, suggested that the rupture the French Revolution introduced was so great that it constituted an insurmountable barrier between an inaccessible past and their own present. He named this present "contemporary" to differentiate it from any other previous present and a future that began to be experienced as progress. This is what Descombes calls the "compréhension modale" of the contemporary (Descombes 1999, p. 22). The French Revolution not only constituted the advent of a new world but also entailed the advent of a new way of experiencing time that was deemed contemporary. Descombes metaphorically expressed this peculiarity that was assigned to the present as "la coleur de contemporanéité" (p. 23). For Koselleck, a paradigmatic example of this historical consciousness occurred in Germany with the appearance of a new expression for recent or contemporary (*neueste*) history, one that seemed to take for granted that the "modern" age was already passed and gone.

Taine's work reflects the epochal quality the present had acquired in France. What is contemporary (*contemporaine*) France? Taine asks this question in the preface to his volume dedicated to discussing the Old Regime. For him, France has replaced, as an "insect" undergoing metamorphosis, the old France with a new one. "Around it, other nations, some more advanced [*précoces*], others less developed [*tardives*], all with greater caution, some with better results, attempt similarly a transformation from a feudal to a modern state; the process takes place everywhere and all but simultaneously" (Taine 1986, p. 13). Comparisons are arranged according to a universal history. "Peoples or states, parts of the earth, sciences, Stände, or classes were found to be in advance of the others" (Koselleck 2004, p. 238). The "contemporaneity of the noncontemporaneous" was possible. The epochal character of the concept of the contemporary was born, and from the beginning, it was vitiated by the legitimation of a civilizational hierarchy that places Europe at the forefront of progress and condemns all other peoples to the "imaginary waiting room of history," in Dipesh Chakrabarty's words (2000, p. 8).

After the French Revolution, the sense of the present as living together changed, now referring to the epochal notion the postrevolutionary present acquired during the nineteenth century. Understood in this way, the present affirms itself by excluding the past. The dead belong to the past. The sense of rupture with the past triggers the extreme action of modifying the calendar. The contemporary present "became a concept for the contemporary epoch opening up a new period and did not simply retrospectively register a past period" (Koselleck 2004, p. 245).

The epochal experience of breaking with the past has had an impact on the development of history as a professional discipline. When the notion of contemporaneity was consolidated in the nineteenth century, history, which was becoming professionalized, separated its own present from its object of study: the past (Rousso 2012, p. 33). Indeed, it is not going too far to say that professional historiography was created in part *through* the gesture of excising the contemporary present from the past. There is a link between temporal experience and history as a discipline, as Jörn Rüsen writes: "History is a specific way in which humans deal with the experience of temporary change. The way they realize it essentially depends upon pre-given or underlying ideas or concepts of time" (Rüsen 2007). Historical knowledge presupposes the established difference between the present and the past. As Kristina Spohr Readman (2011) affirms, "writing scholarly history could not be about one's own experiences and eyewitness accounts but [only about] the systematic examination of surviving written sources from the past" (p. 508). As Pierre Nora (1978) put it, "the exclusion of the contemporary from the field of history is what gives it its specificity ... the very appearance of this historical present coincides with its expulsion from the field of history."

Yet this sense of contemporaneity was not linked to a sense of the past; indeed, the very expression "contemporary history" was regarded during the postrevolutionary era as an oxymoron. History's proper preserve was the past, not the contemporary. Hence, for example, when French minister Victor Duruy introduced contemporary history during the educational reforms of 1865, the concept was ill received by the academic world. The absence of distance, the liveliness of passions, and unfinished processes were some of the criticisms that came from the bastion of a discipline that was considered scientific and professionalized (Phillips 2013; Rousso 2012, p. 67). This idea was clearly expressed by French historian Louis Halphen (1880–1950), who suggested contemporary history is very accessible and open to the legend of the curious, who have little fondness for archives. It became necessary to draw a border between scientific history as it was practiced by university members and as it was practiced by those working in the fields of literature, politics or journalism. Professional history was defined as indirect knowledge gained by proofs and traces. Sources allow the historian to access the unknown world of the past. This distinction between past and present established a division of labor between two disciplines that were becoming professional: history, which looks to the past, and the social sciences, which increase knowledge of the contemporary world. During much of the nineteenth century and the beginning of the twentieth, contemporary history, as a field of study, was rejected by historiographical traditions with Rankean roots (Soulet 1999). Contemporaneity was the self-awareness nineteenth-century European societies possessed. Contemporary was an adjective for a new epoch, a new present, not for the past.

3.2 Contemporary As an Epoch or a Period

Epoch relates not only to an experience of time as it was developed in the previous section, but also to the "historiographical operation," to put it in Certeau's terms, of organizing the past. Daniel Woolf (2023) distinguishes between a period and "the cognitive, hermeneutic, and aesthetic processes of periodizing whereby periods are imagined and imposed on the past by the historian" (p. 51). According to Le Goff, it is the action of cutting time into slices. The result of this action is the construction of an age, epoch, period or cycle.

For Le Goff, the term "period" seems more appropriate; it derives etymologically from the Greek περίοδος (*periodos*), which originally designated a circular path. Between the fourteenth and eighteenth centuries, a period became synonymous with a lapse of time or age, and in the twentieth century, a derivative term, "periodization," achieved currency (Le Goff 2015). Following Jürgen Osterhammel (2006, 2014), Chris Lorenz (2017) calls epochs or periods "blocks of time . . . each of which represents a continuous, coherent unity that is different from the past and future blocks of time" (p. 111). Hence, mainly in France, Germany and Spain, and Latin American countries, especially influenced by France and Spain, at the beginning of the twentieth century, the academic world began to understand the contemporary as the history of the nineteenth century (Aróstegui 2004, p. 42). "Because the nineteenth century is dead" (p. 108) is a phrase that thus demarcates the object of so-called contemporary history – that is, the discipline that focuses on a century that understood itself as contemporary – just as the phrase "medieval history" refers to the period between the fifth and fifteenth centuries in Western history. This is what Vincent Descombes (1999) calls the "epochal conception of the contemporary" (p. 21). It enabled a reconnection of "contemporary" with the past and thus with history; "contemporary history" became an acceptable term, but one principally defined as equivalent to the postrevolutionary period or to the nineteenth century as a whole. It was now understood as a period that includes the contemporary world – the nineteenth century – one that came after the modern world, and in the early twentieth century, first in French degree programs of study in history and then in Spain and Latin American programs, both were included as separated periods: one for the study of modern times and the other for the study of contemporary times. In this epochal conception, contemporaneity is considered "a kind of citizenship of the time" (p. 21).

In Spain, for example, Rafael de Altamira was one of the first to understand how the novelty of the history of the nineteenth century had produced a new historical period (Altamira 1904). Pierre Nora (1988) noted that after contemporary history gained acceptance as the history of the nineteenth century, sufficient time had to pass before "contemporary history was no longer contemporary."

Nevertheless, not all historians, especially Anglo-Saxon authors, subscribed to this idea of acknowledging the nineteenth century as a defined historical period or era. The aftermath of two world wars and the new threat of existential destruction from nuclear bombs seem to have driven some historians away from the remote past to the present, which now seemed more immediate than it had before the war. Barraclough, as mentioned, argued that between 1890 and 1961, such profound changes took place that they constituted true turning points between two eras: an earlier era he calls modern and the next era, which he provisionally designates as contemporary – modern and contemporary in this conception both crept forward chronologically. Barraclough thus intended to differentiate himself from all historians for whom contemporary history did not constitute a separate period with its own characteristics but "rather the most recent phase of a continuous process and . . . simply as that part of 'modern' history which is nearest to us in time" (Barraclough 1964, p. 11). Definitively, for Barraclough, contemporary history "is not merely the latter end of what we call 'modern history'" (p. 12). Aware that the determination of a period should not be merely an external action to those who are living within it and that the two senses of time – *historical consciousness* and *period* – must coincide, Barraclough warned that the historian must not "miss the essential – namely, the sense of living in a new period" (p. 13), something that Taine had experienced but that was lost in the course of the later nineteenth century. Building on this last observation, he warned that "contemporary" was not a very good label, preferring instead to use the term "contemporary history" in a "provisional" way, even if it is "ambiguous and colourless . . . When we can see more clearly the newly emerging constellation of forces, it will be time to think of a term which more nearly represents the world in which we live" (p. 21). However, Barraclough's concerns with respect to the term were not widely accepted.

Many other historians such as Hans Rothfels insisted on bestowing fixed dates on the contemporary. Rothfels designated the year 1917 as the beginning of contemporary history, turning it again into a defined period or "universal-historical epoch" (Rothfels 1953). Gonzague de Reynolds (1957) did likewise, though placing the beginning of the contemporary at the start of the Second World War; they thereby recreated the paradox of holding the contemporary to be *both* a continually moving present *and* a definable period or epoch. But if the contemporary is the present or the recent past, then its edges are constantly renewed as time passes; this cannot happen if beginning and end dates, which, by definition, are fixed, determine a period or epoch. By the early twentieth century, the original sense of *cum tempus* had been completely lost. Two meanings of "contemporary" began to coexist and were mixed: contemporary as present or "the time we are passing through" (Chakrabarty 2004, p. 458), and contemporary as a period.

4 When Contemporary Conflates with Present

Harry Ritter, in the *Dictionary of Concepts in History*, describes the most common scope of the expression "contemporary history," mainly in the Anglo-Saxon sphere: it is "a label for works that deal with the 'recent past' . . . or, more broadly, for studies of any period whose time frame is the historian's own life span" (Ritter 1986, p. 65). Llewellyn Woodward recognizes the diversity of interpretations of the term "contemporary"; however, he prefers for it to designate the present over any other alternative, akin to Kristina Spohr Readman (2011), Gerhard Ritter (1961), Peter Catterall (1997) and R. W. Seton-Watson (1929), among others. "Recent history" is "too vague a term" and "history of our own time . . . is probably the best term, but unfortunately there is no appropriate adjective" (Woodward 1966, p. 1). This last expression is preferred by authors such as Hans Rothfels (1953) and Carlos Navajas Zubeldia (2003, p. 144). Equating the present with the contemporary entails recognizing, as R. W. Seton-Watson (1929, p. 3) pointed out in a lecture delivered at University College, part of the University of London, on December 13, 1928, that contemporary history "changes automatically with the passage of time." In this same sense, and almost a century later, Joel Burges and Amy Elias (2016, p. 3) "assume that 'the contemporary' is a historically deictic term" – that is, one dependent on the temporal position of the person who uses it – and that it is "indicative of a sense of presentness that has been felt by cultures of the historical past as well as those of the current time." This conception of contemporary history presupposes a present moving together with the historian in the timeline or "the idea of fluid temporal boundaries (with a generational component and an openness to constant rejuvenation)" (Readman 2011, p. 514). If we review the collected works of all historians who, until the 1980s, understood contemporary history to be a history of the present or of the recent past, they mostly share three characteristics: (1) All of them frequently invoke Thucydides as the "father" of contemporary history. (2) They account for the emergence of professional history as a developmental process that ended in the nineteenth century. (3) They point out the importance of returning to teaching contemporary history to create citizens who are cognizant of current affairs.

First, *The Peloponnesian War* by Thucydides is often considered the oldest example of "serious" history within the European tradition of historiography, as it concerns events that he lived through (Catterall 1997, p. 447; Henderson 1941; Ritter 1986, p. 65; Seton-Watson 1929, p. 4). As Kristina Spohr Readman (2011) states, "Since the beginnings of what has been considered serious historical writing, history has been indissolubly linked to the present and history's use has always been seen as being a means to improve the understanding of the present ... Similar analogies can also be made with, for example, Guiccardini's, Machiavelli's or Gibbon's work" (p. 509). Timothy Garton Ash (1999) and others such as Peter Catterall (1997), R. W. Seton-Watson (1929, p. 4) and Matthias Peter and Hans-Jürgen Schröder (1994) suggest that from the time of Thucydides "until well into the eighteenth century ... contemporary history was thought to be the best history" (p. xii). The only care that must be taken into account in relation to the "old model of history" is that by the eighteenth century, history had become a "branch of rhetoric and contemporary history that 'cannot be defended on these grounds'" (Catterall 1997, p. 448).

Second, most of these authors consider the birth of a professional history that has the remote past as its object of study to be the result of a gradual process that was institutionally consolidated during the nineteenth century (Schlesinger Jr. 1967). From a historicist point of view, Ritter (1986, p. 65), Woodward (1966) and Arthur Schlesinger Jr. (1967), for example, do not recognize a link between a new experience of time and the birth of history as a discipline in the nineteenth century. In 1967, Schlesinger stated that after Thucydides, "the tendency to regard what was more remote as by definition more 'historical' increased over the next two thousand years ... this tendency was finally institutionalized with the professionalization of history in the nineteenth century" (1929, pp. 69–70). In the same vein, Woodward (1966) affirms that professional history was the result of "learned men who had acquired the particular and very remarkable skill of handling older material" (p. 1), and Ritter (1986) points out that "nevertheless, the PAST, in popular consciousness, gradually became identified with the remote past" (p. 65).

This change was consolidated by the German historical school and caused the present to be separated from the historian's scope. The Rankean school's "ethos" of relying only on written archival documents was exported to the rest of Europe and the United States during the nineteenth century in such a way that "contemporary history was pushed to the fringes of historical scholarship" (Readman 2011, p. 510). Several reasons account for this turn in history toward the remote past. One of them, and the most widespread, was the advance, during the sixteenth and seventeenth centuries, of techniques that allowed scholars to assess the remains of the past "scientifically." "Before the invention of printing and the simultaneous rise of modern states with their record-keeping bureaucracies, written evidence about the distant past was frequently non-existent or at best fragmentary, disorganized, and difficult to obtain" (Ritter 1986, p. 65). It has also been argued that the popularity of newsbooks and eventually newspapers during the seventeenth century produced a sense of an extended present, separate from the events of the past that belonged more clearly to history (Woolf 2001).

Near the end of the nineteenth century, once this entire process had been consolidated, professional historians began to deal only with the remote past, and accounting for the present or the immediate past was dismissed as the task of journalists or publicists. For historian Timothy Garton Ash (1999), this is "a very odd idea: that the person who wasn't there knows better than the person who was" (p. xii). Finally, the popularity of the Rankean school meant that even well into the twentieth century, most historians considered that after an event occurred, a generation or more had to elapse to ensure that an adequate perspective of that event could be formed (Schlesinger Jr. 1967, p. 2).

However, this focus on the past in lieu of the present had, for these historians, strong practical consequences. The wars, new totalitarian forms of power and new technological advances of the twentieth century, which changed the conditions of life, aroused a great demand among the public for a better understanding of recent events. The exclusion of contemporary history from academic study – at least among professional historians – led to the following paradox that Woodward described: "the English governing class, educated mainly at the public and grammar schools and the universities, went into politics or the civil service or the professions knowing less about the state of the contemporary world than they knew about ancient Greece and Rome" (Woodward 1966, p. 2). That is, there was a gap between history and life. "Scholarly history has failed as a guide to life … What was once the pride of the historian … encounters the suspicion of being remote from life and thus fruitless" (Ritter 1961, pp. 261–262). How could it be that the present, which from the beginning (Thucydides) had been the focus of the historian, was now in the hands of journalists and the mass media? In the 1950s, a heated debate took place in the Western world about the relevance of the traditional methods of history to understanding the present. Contemporary history, defined as the discipline that has as its object the recent past or the historian's present, began to be practiced in institutions in Germany, Great Britain, Spain, and the United States in the 1920s.

Most of these historians do not recognize the French Revolution as an event that gave rise to a new experience of time: the experience of a new present as contemporary and its distinction from the feudal past. However, both those historians who acknowledge that history as a discipline emerges from the rupture between past and present, and those – whom we discuss in this section – who believe that the past gradually developed into a distant past object of history, do not consider memory to be the concern of history. Oral history, which emerged after the Second World War and gained significant momentum in the 1960s and 1970s, used individual personal recollection as the primary source for recording what occurred. The function of recollection was to provide information about the experiences of the witness, and its epistemic status was akin to any document, whether written or material. The historian thereby transformed the testimony into historical knowledge. Until the 1980s, the problematic nature of memory was not, in and of itself, a concern for historians, but then the landscape changed.

4.1 Memory and History

In a lecture delivered at the Canadian War Museum on October 31, 2000, historian Jay Winter highlighted the centrality the theme of memory had acquired in the previous two decades. He observed that the term "memory" is not only "the historical signature of our own generation" but is also ubiquitous, although "no one should delude herself into thinking we all use it in the same way" (Winter 2001, p. 66). Referring to history, Winter suggested that "clearly, something important has happened in our discipline, something we need to attend to as more than a passing fashion" (p. 58). If we consider, as Klein does, that memory is a counterconcept – that is, it is part of the repertoire of concepts that help define history – then we can discern that this late twentieth-century turn toward the past, variously described as a "memory boom" (Winter 2006), a "memory surplus" (Maier 1993), a "musealized world" (Huyssen 2007; Lübbe 1983), a "desire to commemorate" (Runia 2007), and the "age of commemoration" (Nora 1989), has helped redefine limits and thereby delimit a new way of understanding history. This diagnosis seemed unanimous; the late twentieth century was a time when the present consumed the past, "a present–past," as if an "extended" present had swallowed the past, which was also expressed as the paradigm of "presence."

From its beginning, history was associated with memory. Among the Greeks, Mnemosyne protected historians from the ravages of Lethe, oblivion. Herodotus presents, in the *Proem* of his *Historia*, the results of his investigations "so that the things made by men are not forgotten in time" (Herodotus 1947). This tradition is maintained by Bacon, who, in the *Novum Organum* (1620), proposes classifying the sciences according to the human faculties: memory, imagination and reason. History belongs to the domain of memory since its purpose is to accumulate materials and collect factual data to allow induction. Bacon's influence is evident in the *Encyclopedia*, edited in the next century by Diderot and d'Alembert, particularly in the *Discours preliminaire*.

Additionally, d'Alembert inserts a "Detailed explanation of human knowledge" where – following Bacon – he places history under the regime of memory. The proposal of Diderot and d'Alembert did not seem to differ from that of Bacon and they were accused of plagiarism. However, aware of the novelty they had introduced, Diderot placed Bacon's disciplinary tree in the *Discours Préliminaire* and urged people to compare them. It was not a matter of things but rather the order of things (Diderot and d'Alembert 1751). Despite the changes from Bacon to the *Encyclopedia*, the affiliation between memory and history is maintained. History is entrusted with the task of storing and safeguarding facts.

The transition between the seventeenth and eighteenth centuries was the time of a famous "quarrel between the ancients and the moderns" and was marked by a wave of skepticism that questioned the scope of historical knowledge. Such criticism was directed mainly at authors, including Saint-Real and Vertot, who distorted historical facts for dramatic or literary effect. The concerns focused on being able to distinguish fact from fable. Hence, Bayle, in his *Dictionnaire*, devastatingly criticizes this mixture of facts and fables and his *Dictionnaire* was an enormous compendium of unconnected facts that have simply been saved from "the ruins of history" (Bayle 1820). Bayle's attack is directed at the use of tradition as the foundation of empirical knowledge.

Voltaire affirms Bayle's skeptical legacy, and following the Lisbon earthquake, he wrote, "The balance in hand, Bayle teaches us to doubt" (Voltaire 1877). In *Le Pyrrhonisme de l'histoire* (1751), Voltaire is responsible for presenting history as either a collection of crimes and misfortunes or as a compendium of lies and fabulous stories. The same skeptical attitude is found in the article *"Histoire,"* which he wrote for the *Encyclopedia*.

The first volume of the *Encyclopedia*, dedicated to Count D'Argenson, appeared in Paris in 1751. On December 28, 1756, Voltaire sent d'Alembert his article "Histoire," fearing that it was "too long" since it is a subject that merits writing "a book" (Voltaire 1756). The author's evaluation is clearly negative. The origins of all history are the stories that parents tell their children and that are transmitted from generation to generation. These accounts are "no more than probable in their origins, as long as they do not collide with common sense, and they lose a degree of probability with each generation" until the truth is completely lost (Voltaire 1756). Therefore, truths in history "are only probabilities," and historians, like judges, "cannot boast of knowing the truth perfectly" (Voltaire 1756). This is Voltaire's critique of a long tradition that associates history with memory. The rupture is found in the very heart of the *Encyclopedia*. From a history derived entirely from memory, we can obtain nothing but probabilities.

This break between history and memory, established by Voltaire within the *Encyclopedia*, was inherited during the nineteenth century, when history was constituted as an academic discipline and understood to be an essentially cognitive activity that seeks to establish – through proof or testimony – an objective and disinterested representation of the past. The separation between past and present became a necessary condition for the constitution of a historical object that was purged of "practical interests." Such a conception excluded the material of memory from historical knowledge as dubious sources that should be subject to verification via historical facts. Memories of lived experiences, including participating historians' own testimonies, were to be treated as documents and evidence and were thus "subject to the same critical examination that a trained historian applies to all his evidence" (LaCapra 2004). Specifically, "written documents seemed less amenable to distortion and thus preferable to memories" (Klein 2000, p. 130). Nineteenth-century historians inherited this rupture between history and memory.

4.2 When Memory Bursts into History

Until the 1980s, memory worked as a counterconcept – that is, one of the limits that helps define what history is not (Klein 2000). The idea that oral testimonies are unreliable because they are the product of memory is reproduced in one of the most famous manuals of the historical method, posthumously published in 1949, *Apologie pour l'Histoire ou Métier d'Historien* (Bloch 1952). Marc Bloch (1886–1944) explains how the criticism of testimonies and historical observation should be carried out. The position of his contemporary Robin George Collingwood (1889–1943) (1994[1946]) is similar, as for both for Bloch and Collingwood, there is no difference between written documents and oral testimonies with respect to how the historian must scrutinize them. We might say that the oral enjoys no epistemological "privilege" over the written. Bloch affirms that testimonies are "expressions of memory" and can always contain mistakes so long as they are affected by emotional factors. He adds that memory becomes incapable of focusing on "those features to which the historian would today attribute a preponderant interest" and that testimonies "do not reach the elemental structure of the past." Both the present and memory act as counterconcepts to professional history. History is about the past, and if the historian considers any oral testimony, then it has to be studied like any other testimony, trace or vestige of the past. Testimonies resulting from the memory of witnesses can be misleading and fallacious, and historians must vindicate them as "proof." The emergence of oral history, autobiography, research on commemoration and ritual, folk history, and other studies that take memory as a central element have not overcome its limits (Urteneche 2022). Eventually, social history provoked a revolution and led historians toward "something often too loosely and vaguely termed cultural memory [but] before 1980, it was rare to see any citations with the word 'memory' in the title" (Blight 2009, p. 241). In these cases, memory was subordinate to the "methodological" treatment of historians and constituted one of the many sources historians used to obtain inferential knowledge of the past.

Even outside of history, the question of memory was at the center of European culture during the transition from the nineteenth century to the twentieth. Indeed, between 1880 and 1925, the works of Freud and Janet in psychology, Stevo and Proust in literature, Bergson in philosophy and Halbwachs in sociology became influential, with discussions emerging first in Vienna and subsequently spreading to the rest of Europe. The appearances of what Ian Hacking (1995) has called the "sciences of memory," anthropology, psychology and sociology, were largely influenced by the problem of memory. In 1925, Halbwachs invented the term "collective memory" and founded *Les Cadres Sociaux de la Mémoire*, which dealt with the sociology of memory.

Yosef Yerushalmi's book *Zakhor* (1982) and Pierre Nora's 1984 introduction, "Between Memory and History," to the *Lieux de Memoire*, published between 1984 and 1992, gave memory a central place. Until then, memory had been the province of psychology or sociology, but now it became visible to historians as a different way to access the past. For Yerushalmi, certain elements of the past – whether mythical or real – are a canonical and shared teaching that must be transmitted. *Halakhah*, which comes from the Hebrew word *halakh* ("to march"), is a set of rites and beliefs that give a people its identity and its destiny. The wise are in charge of transmitting it. History, for Yerushalmi, is an entirely different enterprise; it is neither a collective memory nor a primary source. The past of history is barely recognizable in what collective memory retains. The Jews, for Yerushalmi, are a typical people of memory who only recently adopted history when their traditional means of transmission broke down (see Klein 2000, p. 127): "I tried, with *Zakhor*, to clearly distinguish between collective memory and historiography and to underline the hypertrophy of the latter" (Yerushalmi 1989, p. 25). Moreover, in "Between Memory and History," Nora notes that

> [M]emory and history, far from being synonymous, appear now to be in fundamental opposition. Memory is life, borne by living societies founded in its name. It remains in permanent evolution, open to the dialectic of remembering and forgetting, unconscious of its successive deformations, vulnerable to manipulation and appropriation, susceptible to being long dormant and periodically revived. History, on the other hand, is the reconstruction, always problematic and incomplete, of what is no longer. (Nora 1989, p. 8).

Coming from two different traditions of thought, Yerushalmi and Nora represent the impact of the "memory boom" in history and the defense of its cognitive dimension. While some philosophers and historians maintain what can be called the "classical thesis" in reference to the relationship mentioned in the Greek myth – that is, that history is a form of memory (Herbert Hirsh [1995], D. Blight [2009], Patrick Hutton [1993], Paul Ricoeur [2014], and Dominick LaCapra [2001], for example) – others have defended a discontinuity between the remembered past and the historical past, what we can call the "enlightened thesis," in reference to the rupture Voltaire proposed in the *Encyclopedia* (Yosef Yerushalmi, Arnaldo Momigliano, Pierre Nora, Alejandro Cattaruzza, among others). Within the first group, the positions cover a wide spectrum. For Hutton, historical thought is a result of the mediation between two moments of memory: repetition and recollection. Repetition concerns the presence of the past, the collective memories associated with living traditions; in contrast, recollection refers to a conscious effort to evoke the past. The historical operation consists, then, of the mediation between a received tradition and its critical appropriation: "History is an art of memory because it mediates the encounter between two moments of memory repetition and recollection. . . . Historical thinking mimics the operation of memory in its consideration of the moments" (Hutton 1993, pp. xx–xxi). Hirsch simply identifies history with memory, establishing a direct affiliation with politics. On the other hand, for those who insist on the discontinuity between lived past and historical past, independence must be ensured through a disruptive movement and a critical stance toward tradition: "History and memory have distinct boundaries, and we should maintain them as best as we can. History and memory are two attitudes toward the past. . . . Historians are custodians of the past [memory helps] people imagine their civic lives" (Blight 2009, p. 242). Kenan van de Mieroop (2016) has shown that the debate on the distinction between memory and history is ongoing and remains "a question that is unresolved in scholarship" (p. 13).

This dispute is a result of the "wave of memory" that was experienced together with a confluence of factors. The "age of commemoration," as Nora named it, included the bicentennial of the French Revolution in 1989, the centennial of the Statue of Liberty in 1986 and the Commemoration of the Five Hundredth Anniversary of the Meeting of Two Worlds in 1992, among other events. These commemorative rituals confronted individual and group memories with historical accounts of the past. The case of America was paradigmatic in this regard because Mexico suggested the name "Encounter between Two Worlds" – not the "Discovery of America" or "Día de la Raza," as that date was called until then. This situation forced historians to review what was officially recognized in programs and books in the teaching of history at all educational levels. For Patrick H. Hutton (1993), historians' first focus needed to be on the history of commemoration, but as this sort of work was tied to the postmodern perspective, historians were interested in memory "as a resource in the mobilization of political power, and they were dismissive of the intrinsic value of tradition itself" (p. xv). By the 1980s, collective memory, collective identities, memories and forgetfulness as political phenomena became the main topics not only in history but also in sociology and anthropology. At that time, as Pierre Nora (1997) pointed out, "the influence of memory [was] so strong . . . that the commemorative bulimia of this epoch . . . absorbed even the attempt to master the phenomenon."

This memorial boom in the public space emphasized the opposition of "memory" to "forgetting" and prevailed in multiple national contexts. The Holocaust became the central symbol and the paradigmatic model of a historical memory consciousness. The Holocaust's memory was spread not only in Western Europe but also in North America, the Middle East, Latin America and Africa. Mainly in Argentina and Chile, two countries of the "Cono Sur" (Southern Cone), during the first years of democracy after the dictatorships ended, this "memory boom" gave rise to discourses that showed the existence of plural memories, each of which contained some form of "forgetfulness" and inner disputes concerning hegemonic narratives of the past. So highly success-ful was the concept of using memory in the public sphere that, in Germany, for example, the new term "Memoria-Kultur" entered intellectual jargon as a synonym for "history." For Rothberg (2009), "the emergence of Holocaust memory on a global scale has contributed to the articulation of other histories – some of them predating the Nazi genocide, such as slavery, and others taking place later, such as the Algerian War of Independence (1954–62) or the geno-cide in Bosnia during the 1990s" (p. 6). Thus, Rothberg prefers the concept of "multidirectional memories" to describe the two parallel phenomena: the rise of consciousness of the Holocaust and the political independence of the former subjects of European colonialism, especially in Africa.

In 1998, Allan Megill observed that memory had become "at the present moment, in wide and contentious circulation." David W. Blight (2009) stated that "academic" history demonstrates a "serious gulf between elite knowledge and the huge public interest in the past" (p. 247). Nevertheless, the *Historikerstreit*, the Goldhagen debate, the *Manifesto of Historians* in Chile and the Polish pardon for the Jedwabne massacre, among other events, are examples of historical research in the public sphere that occurred due to a resignification of the meaning of the recent past. If the debates had any consequence, it was their display of how some representations of the past were connected to problems of political and social legitimation in the present.

First, the most important consequence of such debates was that they "sensitized" historians to the relationships they inevitably introduce between past events to give "meaning" to their historical reconstructions. Second, these debates led to a depreciation of historiography as a discursive way to account for the past, based on the awareness that "a pluralism of interpretations" could distort "what really happened."

4.3 Limits of Historical Representation

In 1992, the Czech-American historian Saul Friedländer (1992) published *Probing the Limits of Representation: Nazism and the "Final Solution,"* an edited volume of nineteen chapters, half of them written by historians. As Friedländer announces in his introduction, the purpose that guided the contributions was not addressing specific historical aspects of the Holocaust but rather the shared assumption that they "are dealing with an event of a kind which demands a global approach and a general reflection on the difficulties that are raised by its representation," which puts traditional conceptual categories in check because it is "the most radical form of genocide found in history" (Friedländer 1992, p. 1).

The publication of this book constituted a wake-up call in a discussion that had been taking place since Hayden White's (*Metahistory*, 1973) major intervention in relation to the concept of historiographical representation. Importantly, unlike during the previous stage, it was no longer the literary critics or the philosophers who pointed out the figurative aspects of the plot of history; now, it was the historians themselves who cast doubt on the possibility of representing extreme events of the recent past through the standard means of the historical discipline. Why was it only in the 1990s that historians – at least those studying the Holocaust – questioned the possibility of its historical reconstruction? This urge to prevent the inevitable "meaning" historians would impose on their reconstructions of the past has led many of them to question the moral scope of transcribing (in text) the dimensions of horror, trauma or tragedy historical actors experienced. Thus, in *Probing the Limits*, we find contradictory arguments for a theory of history, for instance that of Carlo Ginzburg, where with only one witness we can know "what happened," versus that of Martin Jay, who affirms that no "negotiation is possible" between the narration of the person who witnessed an event and the historian who reconstructs it.

In this context, two approaches in the controversy – in which not only philosophers or historians participate – regarding the possibility of understanding and historically representing extreme events in the recent past are distinguished. On one hand are those who maintain that these events are knowable and that historians can therefore know them through already established techniques of representation and analyses of the historical discipline (Arendt/ Browning/Goldhagen/Bauman/Todorov). On the other hand are those who affirm that these events cannot be understood, or if they can be, such understanding entails radically new regimes of knowledge and representation (Wiesel/Steiner/Lanzman/Lyotard/Cohen). In general, it is argued that if we understand the past by making sense of data through historical discourse, no discursive model can account for the horror of this kind of crime and the uniqueness of an event in a cognitively and morally responsible way. Wiesel and Steiner, among others, maintain an extreme position within this context – that is, silence is the only moral resource in the face of what they consider unspeakable. Others such as White propose rhetorical resources such as the Latin "middle voice" (White 1992, pp. 37 53) or, like D. LaCapra (2001), resort to conceptual exports from psychoanalysis.

Some, following this same argument, privilege the testimony of the survivors of the events as a form of advantaged access to lived experiences, which facilitates transcending the limits of conventional historiography (Felman/ Laub/Ankersmit/LaCapra). In this context, a survivor's testimony acquires relevance not only for its cognitive dimension but also for its moral scope. In Friedländer's words,

> If one adds the fact that the perpetrators invested considerable effort not only in camouflage, but in the effacement of all traces of their deeds, the obligation to bear witness and record this past seems even more compelling. Such a postulate implies, quite naturally, the imprecise but no less self-evident notion that this record should not be distorted or banalized by grossly inadequate representations. (Friedländer 1992, p. 3)

This "postulate," formulated in the discussion in the 1990s about the limits of historical representation, introduces a gap between what is understood as a factual record of an event and the "representation" or "interpretation" historians make of it. The presupposition is that historiographical discourse introduces an "interpretive" element that "distorts" the "truth" of an account from a witness – that is, from someone who has experienced and observed the facts. We observe at this point a reversal of the role testimony traditionally played in historiographical reconstruction: now, in the "age of testimony," this ceases to be evidence or proof and becomes the *only* way to access the "truth" of the fact. In the words of Shoshana Felman and Dori Laub (1992), "Testimony will thereby be understood ... not as a mode of *statement* but rather as a mode of access to that truth" (p. 16). Understood in this way, the testimony of extreme events occludes the very possibility of historiographical reconstruction, since there is a risk that by integrating testimony into a broader narrative, its truth will be distorted. Given that historical discourse introduces an inevitable mediation between those who did not experience an event and those who did, testimony is the only language through which these extreme events should be represented. Disagreeing with this, Henry Rousso (2016) posits that "a contemporary historian will have to ... create distance with proximity" (p. 22).

Furthermore, history is pressured by the legal sphere. Historians must appear before the justice system, bearing witness to the truth of the so-called crimes against humanity that have been declared inherently non-prescriptive into an imperishable present. (Hartog 2000; Rousso 2012). The historian must appear to tell "the truth." World wars, genocides and incidents of state terrorism, through the legal non-prescriptability of the crimes committed, among other devices, have given rise to an unprecedented phenomenon: the contemporaneity of past crimes with generations who were born after those crimes occurred through the erasure of the temporal distances that separate them. The past does not finish passing; it lives on through mourning, reparation or commemoration.

On the other hand, the search for new theoretical frameworks and methodological tools to account for the magnitude of certain events led some historians to define these experiences as specifically *traumatic* experiences, which authorized them to export analytical categories from psychoanalysis and neurobiology. This turn toward the models of psychoanalysis and neuroscience had strong consequences for both the modalities that were adopted to obtain knowledge of recent traumatic pasts and the discussions around the conceptions of historical time. In the most extreme version, for example, Cathy Caruth (1996), relying on Van der Kolk's (1994) concept of "literal memory," conceives of history as repetition, and from a Freudian psychoanalytic angle, Dominick LaCapra (2001) deems historicity "the return of the repressed." The interpretation of sociocultural phenomena, in psychoanalytic or neurobiological terms, entails the denial of the efficacy of the modern historiographical regime, at least in societies with recent traumatic pasts. The temporality of trauma is incompatible with a historical temporality that presupposes an irreversible "historical past" that is separate and distant from the present regardless of whether the phenomenon of repetition is defined as the return of the repressed or the return of the literal.

5 History of the Present Time

5.1 History "in Crisis"

The scale of the events of the twentieth century also confronted historians with the difficulty of representing a realistic reconstruction of extreme events through the standard procedures of historiography, something questioned from within the historical profession itself (Mudrovcic 2003). The barbarity of what happened undermined the capacity of the conceptual and methodological tools of historiography to make intelligible those events that for some were unknowable and unrepresentable (Wiesel 1985), and what should be understood as "human" was also questioned. The possibility of accounting for an atrocious recent past revealed the limitations of the presupposition of an "intelligible human past."

Together with these transformations, which the historical discipline has been undergoing since the end of the twentieth century, an increasing number of historians, at least those closest to theory, have begun to question in a radical way the basis for historiographical practice. The entry for "histoire" in the *Dictionnaire des Sciences Humain* (Savidan and Mesure 2006), published in Paris in 2006, gives an account of the tensions of the present "historiographical moment" in terms of "an identity crisis," a "time of uncertainties," "an epistemological anarchy," and a "memorial obsession." In 2007, *Manifestos for History* (Morgan, Jenkins, and Munslow 2007) was published. Its editors, after declaring that "history is faltering" and "has lost its way," express their conviction that it is necessary to determine what the discipline should be in the future, since we live "in a society where the rules of the game have changed." Much of this literature refers to the eruption not only of the "memory boom" but also of the new discipline, the "history of the present," which has forced historians to redefine the historiographical field at a conceptual, methodological, and even chronological level. The past is thus losing its quality *as* the past and is being collapsed into the present, becoming a present–past, a past that never passes because it extends into the present. This situation has been reflected in numerous meetings, congresses and journals. In 1984, coinciding with the year of the "dystopian realization" of George Orwell's book, the magazine *Vingtième Siècle: Revue d'histoire* was founded. In its "Declaration of Birth" (Déclaration de Naissance 1984), it declared that it sought to be "a magazine of the contemporary" since the "question of the identity of the present" is a constantly renewed interrogation, thereby questioning the role of the past as an object of history. In 2004, the journal *Temporalités* was founded as a continuation of the *Bulletin Temporalistes*, which was also created in 1984, and it aimed to review the pluralities of temporalities in interdisciplinary projects. In May 2011, a group of leading historians held a workshop at the Freiburg Institute to discuss, as a main focus, "how cultures in general and historians in particular distinguish 'the past' from the 'present' and the 'future.'" The meeting had the (very suggestive) title of "Dissolve Time: Establishing the Borders between the Present, the Past and the Future." In 2010, a colloquium was held in Buenos Aires entitled "The Uses of the Past," a subject that would have been unthinkable several years prior: the past was destined for higher purposes; it was not "used," unless as an example, and it was critically known or gloriously commemorated.[1] The examples multiplied (Alted 1994; Christian et al. 1964; Daddow 2004). Therefore, the feeling became widespread: the paradigm of professional history has become out of tune and has entered a "crisis" (Iggers 2005).

5.2 Presentism and the History of Present Time

The "catastrophes" or "cataclysms" of the twentieth century, due to their traumatic consequences for contemporary societies, defied history's attempts to make them intelligible. The French Revolution, despite the calamities and conflicts it entailed, generated a positive and not painful memory of the past. This was reflected in the notion of progress, in the political projects that were cast into the future and in the rupture the experience of that present established with the past, giving rise to the notion that any events that occurred before 1789 could be treated "historically." The nineteenth century was, in Europe, Latin America and the colonized world, a very violent century with many "catastrophes." Nevertheless, when historians became professional, they separated themselves from their violent present. Although instability and political violence were part of their present, they felt committed to the creation of a new political order: the nation-state. The future commanded it. The history of the present time was unthinkable for a present that established a clear break with its past. The historical past had to be distant and different from the present; this presupposed an irreversible time that prevented the past from being repeated or taken as an example. Historians believed that these characteristics protected them from ethical or political commitments to the present and ensured the objectivity of knowledge. Studying the present, for them, was unthinkable. The present was found in the newspapers, since it was the task of journalists to collect events that had not yet taken "defined forms" and were therefore unreliable. Historians were to be "impartial observers" who did not interfere with the affairs of the present.

For Hartog, the "symbolic" date of 1989 and the fall of the Berlin Wall mark the beginning of the presentist regime. This does not mean that there have not been other crises of time or other temporal experiences. However, at the end of the 1980s, the dominant order of time, at least in Westernized societies, was presentist. The 1980s marked a "crisis" of time that was characterized by "memorial inflation," an inability to project oneself into the future and an oversizing of the present. This was a sign of the presentist "change of epoch"

---

[1] This meeting was organized by Veronica Tozzi at Universidad Tres de Febrero in October 2010.

or of the "slow present," an order of time where the present is permanently installed in a dominant position: "the present is omnipresent." The presentist regime underscored the crisis of the modern historicity regime. According to Hartog, several factors have come together since the 1970s, entailing that salient demands fall on the present: the growth of mass unemployment, the progressive fall of the welfare state, and the increased demands of a consumer society where technological innovation and the quest for profit produce an increasingly rapid obsolescence of things and people. "Productivity, flexibility, mobility: these were the watchwords of the new managers," which led to the desire for and value of the immediate (Hartog 2015, p. 113). New technologies allow transmission in "real time," wars are in "real time," and everything can be consumed in the present. "The present is the only horizon," but, Hartog adds, this occurs alongside a peculiarity: "in the very moment of its occurrence, [the present] seeks to view itself as already history, already past" (Hartog 2015). The last third of the twentieth century produced an "overwhelming, omnipresent present."

At this point, we observe that the "historical past" of historical practice is no longer what it was. All its characteristics have disappeared in a historiography wherein the recent past is entangled with an extended present. The distinction between past and present is obliterated from different angles. The epistemic privilege that a witness acquires prevents the temporal distance that presupposes the retroactive adjustment of the past. The repetitive temporality of the social trauma caused by extreme events imposes the presence of the past in the present and then collapses it with the present. The duty to remember and the mandate not to forget turn the past, once again, into an example to be accounted for, but this time, it is done so that it does not happen again.

The "historical past," in which the herd of historians meekly grazed, as described by Eric Hobsbawm, has been transformed into presence, into a present–past that is part of the omnipresent present. Pessimism concerning the future contrasts with the confident optimism that E. H. Carr, for example, displayed about his discipline in the 1960s: "our conception of history reflects our conception of society . . . declaring my faith in the future of society and in the future of history" (Carr 1983). As developed by Lucian Hölscher (2014), the "concept of the future developed in conjunction with the idea of 'history' . . . no longer constitutes any universal horizon to make sense of" (pp. 225–226). The first issue of the aforementioned *Vingtième Siècle, Revue d'Histoire* (1984) was a thematic number devoted to "Stories of the future," declaring the "official" birth of the history of the present time: "What do we want? To make a magazine of the present. . . Goodbye, History is concluded (*finie*), closed, self-sufficient. Goodbye, linear development of Progress" (Déclaration de Naissance 1984, p. 3).

5.3 History of the Present Time and Institutions

Many institutions were created in the middle of the twentieth century, accompanying the emergence and consolidation of the history of the present time as a discipline in the European context. These national institutions were founded after the Second World War with the main purpose of preserving the resources of the war period. According to Lagrou, "it was an exceptional intervention of the State in historiographical production ... the safeguarding, codification and interpretation of the recent history of war, Nazism and occupation were perceived as a political urgency" (Lagrou 2003, p. 6). In 1945, the Rijksinstituut voor Oorlogsdocumentatie (National Institute for War Documentation) was created in Amsterdam. In occupied Germany, the Deutsches Institut für Geschichte der nationalsozialistischen Zeit (Institute for the History of the National Socialist Period) was founded in 1947 within the framework of the recovery of the archive of the German Ministry of Foreign Affairs, which had been captured by the Allied troops. One of its directors expressed the institution's objective: "Not the writing of history but its documentation is our prime concern" (Montaño, Ortega, and Ovalle 2020, p. 15). Following partition in 1949, that Munich-based institute was later renamed, in 1952, the Institut für Zeitgeschichte (Institute for Contemporary History). In France, Francois Bédarida was the first director of the Institut d'Histoire du Temps Présent (Institute of the History of the Current Age), which the Centre National de la recherche scientifique (CNRS) (French National Center for Scientific Research) created in 1978. This institute replaced the Comité d'Histoire de la Deuxième Guerre Mondiale (CHGM) (Committee for the History of the Second World War), created in 1951. The latter's origins date to 1944, when General de Gaulle's Provisional Government established the Commission on the History of the Occupation and the Liberation of France (CHOLF) to assemble documentary collections and testimonials that were as close as possible to these events (Institut d'Histoire du Temps Présent). This institute is distinct from the Institut d'Histoire Moderne et Contemporaine (Institute of Modern and Contemporary History), also founded in 1978. In Italy, the Istituto Nazionale per la Storia del Movimento di Liberazione (National Institute for the History of the Liberation Movement) was created in 1949; in 1967, this institute was officially recognized by the state. In Austria, the Documentationsarchiv des Österreichischen Widerstandes (Archive of Documentation of the Authentic Resistance) was created in Vienna in 1963 and was endowed with an official status in 1983.[16] Belgium, where any discussion of the history of the occupation was blocked for a long time because of the controversy surrounding the conduct of King Leopold III, created the Center for Research and Historical Studies of

World War II in 1970 (Lagrou 2003, p. 7). In general, these institutions were not located in universities or history departments. In principle, they were meant to ensure the conservation of sources, something that became an "obsession" after the war, primarily in those countries that were occupied, since many people feared that the clandestine activities, which by their very nature left very few traces, would otherwise fall into oblivion. The first years were dedicated to the reconstruction of a collective picture and historical context of the war, excluding considerations of individual responsibilities (Lagrou 2003, pp. 7–8).

Institutions also emerged in other parts of the world, but these were not directly involved in the preservation of documents. The Institute of Contemporary British History was founded in 1986, and in 1988, the Asociación de Historia Contemporánea (Association of Contemporary History), which began publishing the journal *Ayer* in 1990, was established in Spain. In Great Britain, the *Journal of Contemporary History* defined its field of study as Europe in the twentieth century as early as 1966, but three years later, when Belgian historians established the *Revue Belge d'Histoire Contemporaine*, it focused exclusively on the nineteenth century for a long time. In 1993, Josefina Cuesta Bustillo published *Historia del presente* and in 2004, Julio Aróstegui published *La historia vivida: Sobre la historia del presente*, which became a reference for this topic in the Spanish-speaking world. In China, at the end of the 1990s, the Institute of Contemporary Chinese Studies was founded under the tutelage of the Chinese Academy of Social Sciences, created in 1977 (Droit and Reichherzer 2013; Li 2007). The Contemporary History Institute was founded at the University of Ohio in 1987, and its website explains that it "performs a unique function in American higher education today" as it "analyzes the contemporary period in world affairs – the period from World War II to the present – from an interdisciplinary historical perspective" (www.ohio.edu/cas/contemporary-history/about).

In Latin America, especially in the countries of the Southern Cone, the history of the present time has experienced important developments that offer both similarities and differences in comparison with Europe. Unlike in the European context, which concentrated on the Second World War, the interested parties in Latin America focused on issues related to civil–military dictatorships and the transition to democracy. From the beginning of the 1990s to the present, very different processes have taken place in Latin American countries (Capdevila and Langue 2009; Sánchez 2004, p. 261). The progressively public instances of barbarism displayed during dictatorships (torture, disappearances, the kidnapping of children) brought about reflection on the recent past that emulated the debate in Europe about the crimes of the Nazis. This meant that a series of philosophical, epistemological, historiographical and ethical problems emerging from discussion of the Second World War were appropriated for the analysis of Latin American examples, facilitated by the region's strong, long-standing academic links with Spain, France, and Germany, among other countries. These links enabled knowledge sharing following the return of intellectuals and professors from exile in Europe to their countries after democratic regimes took power. In Argentina, like the rest of the South American countries, the investigations first responded to the political needs of the moment and were overseen by specific social actors and human rights organizations.

In the mid-1990s, although publications were already appearing from social scientists, most notably not from historians, the spectrum was dominated by journalistic and testimonial publications. Although non-historiographic works were the most abundant, historians also contributed to this reconstruction (1983–95). In 1994, new investigations and new historiographical essays provided interpretations that began to gradually move away from the previously proposed schemes, and these have multiplied since 2000 (Cattaruzza 2011). As of that year, works on memory and the historiographical reconstruction of the recent past have blossomed in various disciplines (history, sociology, literature), motivating a philosophical and methodological reflection that has complemented from various perspectives the spectrum of publications that were already numerous in 2000. Currently, this field is in the hands of a third generation of historians and, as a result of professionalization and institutionalization, it has become a fully legitimate subject with robust production (Alonso 2010; Cattaruzza 2017; Franco 2020; Franco and Levín 2007). The end of the Uruguayan military dictatorship (1973–85) and that nation's return to democracy were marked by the plebiscite of April 16, 1989, with a very close result (57 percent to 43 percent) in favor of Law 15848, which implied a prohibition on judging those who had committed human rights violations. Twenty years later, on October 25, 2009, another referendum ratified it again. In 2011, Congress nullified it. The historiography of the first years of the new civil regime was not homogeneous in terms of the problems, approaches and topics studied. Two trends were prevalent: (1) the concern to present, in an organized way, short and fast-reading texts that provided basic knowledge about national history and were not vitiated by the dictatorial approach; (2) the strongly felt and quickly abandoned need to study the dictatorial process (Montaño 2015; Soler 2000). From 2005 to the present, Uruguayan historiographies of the recent past flourished, concerning not only the military dictatorship but also the experience of exile, the role of the church, the interference of the United States, and the impact of the student movement (Bohoslavsky 2010; Montaño 2015, p. 43). In Chile, the development of the history of the present time was also marked by the nation's dictatorial past (1973–90). Historian Dany

Monsávez Araneda, assessing national historical production in 2016, finds that the field of Chilean history is still at a formative stage if it is compared with Argentina. There are two causes: a scarcity of resources and a lack of financial support. The development of the new political history has contributed to the history of the present time, which has made it possible to incorporate developments from other disciplines such as economics, social sciences, and cultural history (Araneda 2016). A particular perspective that acquires this discipline in Chile is the study of the past as a form of heritage. "Local heritage" and "heritage from below" are two means of access to the past that would replace the social memory in the sense that historical and cultural memories are transformed into merchandise. It is a commodified memory (Aravena 2009, 2014).

In Brazil, the growth of this disciplinary subfield was also accompanied by a return to democracy. In the 1980s, the period of political opening, an increasing number of investigations were created both in universities and in institutions charged with preserving memory. In its beginnings, the history of the present time in Brazil was stimulated by oral history, a disciplinary field that was established in 1975, overseen by the Fundação Getúlio Vargas (Getúlio Vargas Foundation) in Rio de Janeiro and strengthened with the creation of the Associação Brasileira de Historia Oral (ABHO) (Brazilian Association of Oral History) in 1993. In 1994, the first Laboratório de Estudos do Tempo Presente (TEMPO) (Laboratory or Present Time Studies), which belonged to the Instituto de História da Universidade Federal do Rio de Janeiro (Institute of History of the Federal University of Rio de Janeiro) was founded (Müller and Iegelski 2018). In 2011, a truth commission to investigate political crimes against human rights was created and the Lei de Acesso à Informação Pública (Law of Access to Public Information) was enacted in 2011. In 2013, the Seminário Internacional do Tempo Presente (International Seminar on the Present Time) was held, organized by the Programa de Pós-Graduação en História da Universidade do Estado de Santa Catarina (UDESC) (Graduate Program in History, State University of Santa Catarina), whose latest edition took place in 2023. All these actions led to an explosion of studies that concerned not only the victims of the military regime but also Afro-Brazilian people and indigenous groups who had suffered exploitation and discrimination (Avelar and Pereira 2018; Cezar 2012; Falcon 2013; Ferreira 2018; Pereira 2015; Varella 2012).

The hegemony of the Annales School in Mexican historiography during the 1990s is one of the reasons for the delay in incorporating the account of state violence in the past forty years (Garmiño Muñoz 2020). Since 2000, the political change in Mexico following decades of single-party rule by the

Institutional Revolutionary Party (IRP) has contributed to historians incorporating the violence of the present into their narratives (Dutrénit and Varela 2010) and addressing its epistemological and methodological challenges (Gamiño 2011; Nava 2015). Eugenia Allier Montaño recently pioneered the consolidation of the field of the history of the present time through the creation, in 2012, of the Institutional Seminar on the History of the Present Time (UNAM) and the organization, in 2017, of the Red de Investigación Nacional sobre la Historia del Tiempo Presente (National Research Network on the History of the Present Time). The truth commission is a very recent initiative (2021) in Mxico, and its aim is to shed light on the human rights violations committed between 1965 and 1990.

5.4 Many Names for the Same Historiographical Field?

F. Bédarida coined the phrase "history of the present time" to describe the focus of the institute the CNRS created in 1978. This name stemmed from a combination of circumstances. First, the new institute had to be distinguished from the Institute of Modern and Contemporary History, created during that same year. In France, there was a tradition of teaching contemporary history courses, but this was understood as covering the history of the nineteenth century, so it was necessary to differentiate the "present" from the "contemporary." "How could we think that we were contemporary with Robespierre or Napoleon? Hence, the radically ambiguous term 'contemporary history' is replaced by the expression 'present time'" (Bédarida 1998). Second, the term "present time" reflects Bédarida's reading of Henri-Irénée Marrou (1904–77). Marrou, far from considering the distance from the past as a given fact, defined historiographical operation as a dialectical relationship between past and present. Any "distance" is produced by historians, according to Henri-Irénée Marrou (1954). Third, P. Garcia, a historian at the institute, suggested that at that time, this type of history was responding to social demands not only for the memorial era and its commemoration but also for justice – for historian witnesses, minority groups, and so forth. In 1982–3, F. Bédarida's seminar was dedicated to "L'histoire du temps présent et ses usages: recherches fundamentale appliqué." H. Rousso, who became the director of the institute in 1994, insisted on the importance of this last dimension even more strongly than his predecessors (Garcia 2010). In relation to the term "present time," Bédarida also affirmed that he preferred it to another expression, "historia immédiata, histoire immédiate," which was more common at that time. Since 1963, the Seuil publishing house had begun releasing, under the direction of Jean Lacouture, a series of works focused on the 1930s and the prewar era, which were brought together in the collection known as *Histoire Immediate*. Bédarida suggested that the word "present" had more heuristic power in relation to the present/past pair, and that such power was totally absent from the concept of immediacy (Bédarida 2001, p. 154). In a work published in 2016, Henry Rousso (2016) asks:

> Why are there so many different notions to describe what appears to be the same historiographical field: histoire contemporaine, histoire du temps présent, or histoire immédiate in French; contemporary history, modern history, or even instant history in English; Zeitgeschichte, neuere or neueste Geschichte in German; historia vivida or pasado vivo in Spanish; tempo presente in Portuguese?

Although differences and similarities can be noted among all these concepts, they all try to express the dimension of coetaneousness that is implicit in the concept of contemporary history but without confusing this expression with the term that was traditionally identified with the revolutionary break of 1789 (Bustillo 1993; Garcia 2003). In Latin America, to avoid this confusion, the terminology "recent history" has come into usage.

5.5 Criticism and Controversies

Since its inception as a subdiscipline, the history of the present has aroused controversy. Years later, in relation to the foundation of the institute, Bédarida pointed out "that a renowned historian such as Gérard Noiriel has severely criticized the practices of the Institute's researchers. His reproaches had to do with making an 'évènementielle' history, forgetting the longue durée . . . one should proceed differently to make a truly contemporary history . . . and not fall into a political illusion" (Bédarida 2001, p. 154). Bédarida identifies two "minor" objections that can be called "epistemological." The first of them concerns the "holy" notion of "distance" that seemed to be a sign and guarantee of the objectivity and scientific nature of history, which are, for him, a fiction. Since no one can escape their own subjectivity, history must be more "cautious" when approaching more recent periods. The second objection concerns the lack of archival material. Although some states postpone the opening of archives, there are other types of sources, as oral history has shown. Nevertheless, there is an objection that, for Bédarida, is a "true" objection – an ontological objection – concerning historical time and how the present is experienced. The history of the present time analyzes and interprets "a time of which he knows neither the concrete result nor the end of processes" (Bédarida 1998, p. 24). The "ignorance of tomorrow" and the work on processes that are still "not closed" and prevent the "retrospective illusion of fatality" favor the field of the possible and help Garcia, as P. Ricoeur suggested, to "unfatalize history" (Garcia 2018, p. 2).

However, a historian of the present time, more than any other, should keep in mind that "all historical construction is provisional" and can be corrected in the future. In 1998, François Bédarida (1998) indicated that "the battle is won, since this historical field is fully recognized as the territory of the historian and its cognitive and heuristic value is admitted" (p. 20).

The problem of delimiting scope must also be added to these criticisms. In 1976, P. Nora, director of the École des hautes études en sciences sociales (EHESS) (School for Advanced Studies in the Social Sciences), realized that the history of the present time implied a real rupture in French historiography; it is a history that in order to exist must exclude the "contemporary" (understood as the nineteenth century), hence its specific character. The various definitions mostly relate to chronologies, events or generations. The use of chronology usually defines the field of study in relation to access to oral testimonies. Denis Pechanski, Michael Pollack and Henry Rousso affirm that the history of the present time covers "a historical sequence marked by two moving beacons. Consequently, this sequence goes back almost to the limits of a human life … by living witnesses." In 1998, referring to the practice carried out at the IHTP, Bédarida (1998) stated that "it has been to consider the time of lived experience as the present tense … It is truly a question of shifting ground, with more or less elastic periodizations" (p. 22). This chronological criterion has been strongly criticized in the French sphere by M. Trebitsch (Aróstegui 2004, p. 48) and in the Latin American sphere by Marina Franco and Florencia Levín. Julio Aróstegui (2004) and María Inés Mudrovcic (2005) prefer to appeal to a generational criterion. Thus, the history of the present time is a historiography whose object is events or social phenomena that constitute memories of at least one of the three generations that share the same historical present. This recourse to generations has been criticized for not being centered on processes or events. As noted earlier in this Element, Henry Rousso suggests that the beginning of the history of the present, as it is called in France, invariably begins with "the last catastrophe" – that is, with the last extreme and unprecedented case of violence, typically political in nature. Rousso adopted this expression from Heimpel:

> "Any present time begins with the latest catastrophe, the most recent one." This rather provocative definition comes from Hermann Heimpel, a German medievalist who was director of the Max Planck Institut für Geschichte in the late 1950s and a former professor at the Reichsuniversität of Strasbourg when the French city was under German rule during the Nazi era. (Rousso 2016, p. 18).

As a result of this situation, "what historians call 'contemporary history' changes constantly" (Rousso 2016, p. 18). We can agree with Sarah Maza (2017) and Daniel Woolf (2023) that

It may reasonably be asked if the fixation in Western historiography on crises, traumatic and violent "turning-point" events such as wars, revolutions and battles, which provide tempting starting and stopping points for our accounts of the past, are not a by-product of a global historical culture that until relatively recently has been highly Eurocentric in its practices and fixated on political units, especially the nation-state. (Woolf 2023, p. 36)

In 2000, Rousso identified the year 1945 as the beginning of the present time because of the establishment of the welfare state, the emancipation of women and the radical transformation of international relations that occurred then (Droit and Reichherzer 2013; Rousso 2000). Other scholars have argued that it is the effects of these catastrophes, generally read in terms of trauma, that characterize the field of competence of this type of historiography. Summarizing some major elements of the practice of contemporary history in the present day, Henry Rousso specifies four characteristics: First, "there is the presence of the actors of history, whether or not they testify about their own experience. [He] emphasizes here the notion of the 'actor of history' and not that of the 'witness' as historians usually do" (Rousso 2016, p. 26). He considers that it is "the major singularity of a contemporary history." Second, "there is ... a structural link between writing contemporary history and dealing with the effects of historical traumas. In a certain sense, contemporary history (or the histoire du temps présent, in French) are direct consequences of the collective traumas of the twentieth century" (p. 27). Third, "there is the central question of the event, and the necessity to rehabilitate the short-term perspective" (p. 27). Fourth, "law and justice became major vectors of memory and major narratives on the recent past, especially in the context of the 'historical trials,' from Nuremberg to the recent tribunals for Rwanda or the former Yugoslavia" (p. 27). However, another phenomenon is present in the history of present time. At first glance, it would seem that the only pasts that are present are recent pasts. Concepts such as "traumatic pasts," "extreme pasts," "pasts that do not pass," "literal pasts," and "past–present" have been used, with greater or lesser success, to analyze phenomena such as the Shoah, the Armenian genocide, and Latin American state terrorism, among others. Nevertheless, there are events, such as slavery or the genocide of indigenous peoples, that are distant in time but are still "alive" and instrumental when trying to create a deep political self-understanding of the present. Those pasts that have not yet passed although distant in time are "in conflict" with the present, and they point to what we might call the present's temporal density (Mudrovcic 2009, p. 14). Indigenous peoples, for example, do not belong to the past, nor should their remains be held in natural history museums. Their past is present and only very recently have they themselves begun to be considered by the practitioners of the history of the present time (Avelar and Pereira 2018; Mandrini 2007).

In 2013, the German historian Franz Reichherzer and the French historian Emmanuel Droit published an article in *Vingtième Siecle: Revue d'Histoire* (one of the leading journals concerned with the history of the present time) wherein they advocated leaving behind what they consider a "historical singularity." They encouraged abandoning what they call the "drunk ship of the present time" for three reasons. The first is to exit the "tyranny of the national." By this they do not refer to the dissolution of writing about the national in an era of global and connected history, but rather "they deplore the focus on the national framework to reconsider the question of identity" (Droit and Reichherzer 2013). The nation-centered character of the history of the present time is reflected not only in the editorial field but also in historiography. The second reason is that we must exit "a history centered on the violence of war." This fact is evident mainly in the stagnation of the discipline of political history. Finally, they appeal to historians to abandon "the search for the 'last catastrophe.'" Given that the subject's first investigations were marked by what has been called the "era of catastrophes," the investigations were tied in Europe to the world wars and their medium-term consequences and in Latin America, fundamentally, to the military dictatorships. This has entailed the problem for these authors that "the historical caesuras that frame the period are mobile" (p. 136) and focus only on catastrophes, but many other issues remain unaddressed (p. 138). The authors propose abandoning the singularity of the present time centered on the medium term and associated with the "journalist's time" and advocate a "social history–science of the present." This implies "leaving the conception of a present time defined as a short time and thinking of history as a science of humans inserted in multiple layers of pasts present in the present" (p. 144).

Contrasting and almost disobeying this Franco-German request to "abandon ship," in Latin America, the history of the present time is a "vivid matter." In 2020, a group of Mexican academics led by Eugenia Allier Montaño, César Ortega and Camilo Vicente published the book *En la Cresta de la Ola: Debates y Definiciones en Torno a la Historia del Tiempo Presente* (*On the Crest of the Wave: Debates and Definitions concerning the History of the Present Time*). Although the project was conceived in Mexico, the book brings together twenty essays by historians, social scientists and philosophers, most of them Latin American and a few of them European. The book constitutes an excellent review of the state of this discipline and an example of the strength that the history of the present time has in Latin America. However, with cautious enthusiasm in their final reflection, the editors point out that although in the future this part of the historiographical field could disappear, simply having forced historians to turn their eyes to the present justifies its existence. In 2023, the UDESC successfully hosted the Seminar on Contemporary History, which garnered widespread participation. The event drew theorists and historians not only from Latin America but also from Europe.

6 Absolute Time, Chronology, and History

If we pay attention to the debates surrounding the different denominations that the history of the present time has received or the various dates proposed as the "beginning" of the present, we will notice that these discussions are infused with the presupposition of a linear, chronological, and universal concept of time. This temporal assumption is articulated quite effectively by Hartog when, in an interview conducted by the historian Pablo Aravena during his visit to Chile, he affirms:

> Indeed, what does it mean to live in a presentist regime? It means that we exist immersed in events that come one after another but lack any connection between them, and all we can do is act swiftly, react. Behind this lies the certainty that we have entered an era of catastrophes … an earthquake, a plane crash, a flood, an epidemic, a nuclear accident. However, there is no link between them. (Aravena 2022, p. 28)

I want to emphasize two phrases that give us a clue about the concept of time and the present underlying Hartog's statement: (1) "we exist immersed in events that come one after another" and (2) "there is no link between them." The phrase "exist immersed" presupposes a concept of the present as an *external time* to events and *in* which they happen. The present would be the current portion of time, an absolute, natural, external medium in which events occur. Chakrabarty clearly expresses this idea of present as "the time or period we are passing through" (Chakrabarty 2004, p. 458). This understanding of time and consequently of the present stems from the Newtonian conception that served as the temporal framework not only for the social sciences but also for the physical–natural sciences such as biology or geology. These sciences, in turn, organized their "toolboxes" (methodologies and conceptual apparatus) during the nineteenth century to comprehend and "read" the world. "The new academic field of history took for granted a chronological time as a neutral medium within which events occur and treated history as a continuum along which people, nations, or civilizations moved" (Wilder 2022, p. 147).

This universal, linear, and chronological concept of time underlies the notion of contemporaneity when understood as (a) an epochal experience, (b) a period, or (c) simply the present as the time we are currently going through. These assumptions of linearity and chronology give rise to different ontological and epistemological problems in each case: the exclusion of the "other" in the epochal experience of contemporaneity or what Johannes Fabian (1983) referred to as "alochronism" in the field of anthropology; the challenge of "temporal distance" and the epistemological demand for "objectivity";

anachronism; the plurality of dates marking the "beginning," at different points along the timeline, of the present in the history of the present, or the issues of incommensurability and the multitude of temporal scales when the present confronts phenomena like the Anthropocene.

The conception of absolute, homogeneous time, which is external to events, linear, and flows constantly and gradually from past to present, gradually took shape (Tanaka 2019, p. 31). The notion of abstract and universal time emerged in Europe through a process that Le Goff (1980) dates back to the twelfth century. When Newton formulated his idea of universal time in the seventeenth century, many transformations of different times (natural cycles, religious time, social festivities, among others) had already occurred. The novelty was conceiving a time independent of times related to the moon and stars, human activities, and other natural regularities. "Absolute, true, and mathematical time, of itself, and from its own nature flows equably without regard to anything external, and by another name is called duration. Relative, apparent, and common time, is some sensible and external" (Wilcox 1987, p. 22). Toward the end of his life, Newton wrote works dedicated to chronology, in which his interest was focused on dating and precisely locating events. These works had an impact on history because they enabled any event to be precisely placed on a timeline that stretches infinitely backward and forward (p. 209).

This chronological and abstract concept of time enabled the organization, arrangement, and control of events through devices such as calendars and clocks, freeing them from the constraints of social, biological, or astronomical time. The naturalization of clock time and the standardization of time contributed to new conceptions and experiences of shared public time detached from natural rhythms and specific tasks (Wilder 2022, p. 143). Moishe Postone describes this process as a shift from concrete time to abstract time (Postone 1993, pp. 186–225). Through this process time began to appear to be a natural phenomenon independent of human action (Elias 1992). This temporal conception enables historiography to divide and organize the timeline into successive periods or epochs, among which "the decision to be different or to no longer be what has been up to that point (Renaissance, Revolution)" is made (Certau 2007, p. 17). History reaffirms a temporality in which categorical distinctions between past, present and future are considered natural and "unbridgeable" (Wilder 2022, p. 146). Tanaka points out this contradictory feature of modernity: while abstract and mathematical time unifies, history fragments it into past, present, and future, and classifies it into periods or epochs. Newtonian duration between two moments – before and after – becomes spatialized (Tanaka 2019, p. 94). The historian's goal is to account for social change, and it takes place *in* time.

This way of conceiving time also presupposes a substantialist ontology, meaning that events are "things" or "occurrences" (substances) that happen and that we can relate or not, like the earthquake, the epidemic, the plane crash, and Hartog's nuclear accident. Time is the medium in which what historians call "facts" occur: the medium in which societies, nations, and peoples develop and in which historians relate events in processes through which they explain how they came to be what they are today. It is the medium that allows for what Zoltan Simon (2019) calls a developmental view or what Mandelbaum (1967) designates as "historicism": "the belief that an adequate understanding of the nature of any phenomenon and an adequate judgment of its value can be achieved considering such a phenomenon in terms of the place it has occupied and the role it has played within a development process" (p. 24).

Arthur C. Danto's *Analytical Philosophy of History*, first published in 1965, serves as an excellent example of these temporal presuppositions. Danto's book made a significant contribution to the long-standing debates in the philosophy of history, particularly centered on issues of explanation that spanned decades. It not only engaged with the traditional and more purely "historiographic" dialogues on historical "method," but also intersected with the emerging discussions in the 1970s about the role and function of narration in the discipline. Danto considers narration a form of explanation (Danto 1985, 201–232). There, Danto offers a conception of what he understands as constituting the historical past. His intention is not to address directly the "historical past," but rather, the past as it emerges from the temporal articulation of "narrative sentences" that, according to Danto, relate in a particular way to historical knowledge. The historical past presupposes a time as a linear succession in which events occur; a separation and distinction between past, present, and future; a flow from the future to the past; and temporal irreversibility. These temporal conditions are necessary but not sufficient to establish a historical past. For the historical past to be possible, the historian, from a present within the temporal continuum and, of course, without knowledge of how future events will unfold, describes past events in relation to other events that are also in the past but are future in relation to the ones being described. The result of this teleological–retrospective temporal relationship is the "historical past." The one or multiple historical pasts conceived in this way necessarily imply the epistemic privilege of the historian over the witness and the historian's lack of knowledge about certain future developments. Danto uses the metaphor of a container:

> Let the past be considered a great sort of container, a bin in which are located, in the order of their occurrence, all the events which have ever happened. It is a container which grows moment by moment longer in the forward direction, and moment by moment fuller as layer upon layer of events enter its fluid, accommodating maw. (Danto 1985, p. 146).

Time becomes a quantitative measure that determines, from the past to the present, the constitutive distance of the epistemic principle of objectivity, differences, and relationships. This chronological, irreversible, and linear time allows events to be organized from "behind" to "ahead." As Certau (2007) says, "History, then, unfolds at the borders where a society connects with its past and with the act that distinguishes it from it" (p. 53). The past, as a result of the "historiographic operation," must be discovered retrospectively through evidence – as the outcome of inferential knowledge. This notion of temporal linearity, universality, and homogeneity is presupposed in history, and as Hartog aptly reflects in his 2013 interview, we are immersed in events that come one after another, and we can choose whether or not to connect them.

6.1 The Present within the Framework of Linear and Chronological Time: Some Problems

The idea Newton introduced of the chronological and linear universality of abstract time that "flows uniformly unrelated to any external thing" differs from both Jacques-Bénigne Bossuet's universality and Immanuel Kant's universality. The universality of Bossuet's sacred time did not imply the adoption of a single and simultaneous chronology. Neither Bossuet nor Pascal possessed the idea of chronological universality "external" to events: although, from our perspective, two peoples lived simultaneously, they did not coexist synchronously in the same time. Alain de Libera (2000) clearly expresses the idea of multiplicity of times in the Middle Ages. "The Baghdad of the third century of the Hegira and the Aix of the ninth century of the Christian era are contemporaries, but they are neither in the same time nor in the same world or in the same story." For the historian of medieval philosophy, there is 'a multiplicity of durations: a Latin duration, a Greek duration, an Arab-Muslim duration, a Jewish duration" (pp. 15–16). Each cultural world has its own peculiar time. A multiplicity of times coexisted in Medieval Europe that also coexisted with the peculiar times of American or African peoples with whom they had no interaction (Mudrovcic 2019, p. 463). The absence of a universal chronology is also present in Immanuel Kant's idea of universal history. In *Idea for a Universal History with a Cosmopolitan Purpose* (1784), the universal is the plan or system of nature that unfolds systematically at different times or stages, and the philosopher discovers it in the multiplicity of absurdities of human things (Kant 2017).

Two characteristics define the novelty introduced by the contemporary present experienced by nineteenth-century people. First, that contemporary present presupposes a universal time that is incompatible with other temporal frames. It is the "now" of a temporal continuum from which past and future are distinguished and must be realized in relation to the totally of the continuum itself. Second, it discriminates in the same present: not all that exists at the same time belongs to the contemporary present. "Being contemporary in the nineteenth century means belonging to a homogeneous class whose characteristic is to have left behind a feudal past" (Mudrovcic 2019, p. 466) – that is, not every coeval shares the same present. A political norm is introduced in the universal chronological time discriminating both diachronically and synchronically. The so-called temporal rupture between past and present is normative. Continuous and absolute time remains indifferent to the norm. Comparing France – and then the West – with other nations from the point of view of their political development, Taine considers that although they coexist with it, they are not all "contemporary" – some are "more advanced"; others are "less developed." Added to this synchronic discrimination was diachronic discrimination: the past only belongs to the dead who have contributed to the new political order. That is why "peoples without history" are possible. The contemporary present, as an epochal consciousness, was born infected with what Fabian (1983) much later, and in relation to anthropology, referred to as "allochronism" or "denial of coevalness ... the persistent and systematic denial to place the referent of anthropology in a Time other than the present of the producer of anthropological discourse" (p. 31). Even though the present might lack "la coleur de contemporanéité" from the nineteenth century, it can take on other normative dimensions that delineate to whom the present belongs. Ernst Bloch, for example, in 1932, in the first edition of *Heritage of Our Times* (*Erbschaft dieser Zeit*), states that neither the youth of the bourgeois nor the peasantry are "in step with the barren Now." For Bloch, the peasantry more properly belonged to the past than to the present, modern capitalist world. The peasants and the petit bourgeois are non-contemporaneous (*Ungleichzeitigkeit*) with the present. The synchronicity of the asynchronous was possible, and with it, the expulsion of the other from the present. The norm allows the "temporal comparisons" in qualitative terms: that is to say, "temporal comparisons" have a strong evaluative component in considering the objects of study over their different stages of development (Steinmetz, Simon, and Postoutenko 2021, p. 455). The backwardness of Latin America as "feudal" produces the qualitative "temporal distancing" from "advanced" European countries (Grosfoguel 2000). That qualitative "temporal distancing" is what Fabian called "allochronism."

But contemporaneity also, when taken as a concept of epoch or period – the result of the "historiographical operation" of organizing the past – presupposes a universal linear matrix in which it is positioned as the *last* of the periods. Organizing epochs through dynastic successions or through considerations such as metals or sacred texts entails the establishment of time based on qualities that express the characteristics of a period, completely independent of a single temporal framework. The perfection of artistic achievement and the remarkable feats of the human spirit led François-Marie Voltaire (1954[1751], 7) to select "four centuries in the history of the world," with the century of Louis XIV the embodiment of felicity. In Voltaire's perspective, the age of Louis XIV stands as "the most enlightened that ever existed." For Voltaire, the distinctive "perfection of the arts and greatness of the human spirit" drive the selection of these specific centuries, leaving out others. Unlike the chronological principle that defines the "contemporary" as the *last* period, Voltaire's organizational principles for the "centuries" do not assume a linear time, an absolute and an universal time, an irreversible or a simultaneous chronology, which allowed for anachronism. Chronology serves as a record of both the uninterrupted progression of uniform time and the sequential progression of history through distinct periods. "Viewed either way, anachronism refers to the error, both logical and empirical, of conflating a given past with a given present" (Wilder 2022, p. 148).

At the end of the nineteenth century, universal time was spatialized. In 1884, in Washington DC, the International Meridian Conference established that "it was desirable to adopt a single global meridian to replace the many that coexist and that all countries should adopt a universal day" (International Meridian Conference 1884). When the global meridian was adopted, the Western BC/AD dating system, which was used for the first time by the monk Bede by around 731, and Newtonian absolute time were imposed all over the world: "The same dating system can locate such distant events as the battle of Marathon, the period when people first engaged in agriculture, and even the time when life on the earth began" (Wilcox 1987, p. 7).

Contemporary as the *last* period and contemporary as the *actual* present we are passing through were both thought possible. Both types of "presents" entail the universality of a geographical linear time matrix and the universal chronological simultaneity. Although Europeans were liberated from the specific normative dimension the present had acquired during the nineteenth century, in Europe itself, it remained the norm that structured the global historical time "first in Europe, then elsewhere" (Chakrabarty 2000, p. 7). The present began to be understood as the current segment of a universal timeline – that is, a present that moves along with the historian's timeline from which the historian retrospectively "constructs" a period that they label, for instance, contemporary. This present, as Readman (2011) pointed out, presupposes "the idea of fluid temporal boundaries" (p. 514), a concept that allows multiple events located in different points of the timeline to serve as the "beginning" of the present, often collapsing between them. Despite the criticism that the conflation of political history and "event-based" history has

received, it is the events, rather than major economic, social, or cultural transformations, that have structured historical time (Assis 2023). "It is not the first Industrial
Revolution that launches the contemporary period in the French tradition, but
rather the French Revolution" (Rousso 2016, p. 175). Assuming, then, that the
"beginnings" of the contemporary period accept variable criteria, Rousso lists
a series of dates that, on the linear timeline, would "inaugurate" the present: the
already classic year of 1789 in the French tradition, a rupture that became obsolete
in 1980 with the emergence of the history of the present time; 1917, or rather, the
sequence 1917–18, especially in German historiography; 1945, for the English
tradition; 1940, with the outbreak of World War II; 1989–2001, with the fall of the
Berlin Wall. Embracing the full linearity and chronology of historical time, Rousso
concludes that the present in any history of the present time is not only an "after"
but also an "aftermath" of the last political catastrophe of each country (p. 189).

The temporal linear continuum also allowed the idea of the temporal distance
to be conceived in quantitative terms to the extent that the past "moves away"
from the present, and the epistemological idea of the objectivity is forged
through the historian's connection with the "remote past." Chris Lorenz aptly
captures this notion of a distant past and its counterpart, historical objectivity:
"According to professional historians, it is the progress of time that causes the
passions of the witnesses to cool off by producing temporal distance. And it is
this temporal distance that enables professional historians to develop their
superior insights over testimonial evidence by using the benefits of hindsight"
(Lorenz 2014, p. 35). Temporal distance was paired with historical objectivity.
This idea is clearly expressed in 1931 by Johan Huizinga, who responded, when
colleagues and friends asked him to give a course on contemporary history:

> Lecturing on the recent past, no, I have nothing to say about that they [my
> students] cannot read in the papers. What they need is distance, perspective,
> well-defined historical forms, and the eighteenth century is actually much nicer
> and more important, I do not say than the present itself, but than the imperfect
> and unreliable historical image [*historiebeeld*] that one can form of it.
> (Huizinga 1990, II, p. 343)

Writing of contemporary history or a history that focuses on a past very "close" to
the present is not a reliable task. This was why the teaching of contemporary
history faced so much resistance. The recent past was deemed inappropriate for
historical research, as the quantitative "proximity" – measured in years – in the
timeline of events could lead to a biased and self-interested understanding of
them. The historical past had to be understood "in itself," stripped of any practical
relevance it might hold for the present. However, the quantitative temporal
distance, which once seemed to guarantee objectivity and shielded historians

from becoming entangled in historical events, is invalidated from the history of the present time. One of the unquestioned temporal foundations of its own discipline – temporal distance – has entered a crisis. Historical temporality has ceased to be a presupposition and is now debated within the discipline itself. The "temporal distance" is transformed in a focal point of analysis in the theme issue *Historical Distance: Reflections on a Metaphor* of the journal *History and Theory*, in December 2011. The "memory boom," its impact on the temporal framework of history, and the emergence of history of the present time have highlighted the permeable boundaries between the past and the present. Concepts such as presence (Bevernage 2012; Lorenz 2010; Runia 2014), trauma (Caruth 1996; LaCapra 2001; Langmuir 1990), revocation (Bevenage 2012), and hauntology (Kleinberg 2017), among others, attempt to account for the presence and enduring persistence of the past in the present. However, despite these concepts revealing recurrent, circular, or even collapsing connections between the past and the present, they retain elements of a "modernist" notion of time, as Lorenz suggests, functioning as a "containertime" that encompasses all other temporal dimensions. Even when considering the present as saturated with the past, it is often envisaged as an integral part of a uniform container, distinguishing one present temporal block from another past one (Lorenz 2021).

6.2 "Living Together": A Relational Approach of Understanding the Present

Despite the criticisms that the homogeneous, absolute, and linear concept of time has received, which has become the chronological "idol" of the Western world, at least in the social sciences and humanities, and even though scientific conceptions of time have radically challenged our ways of understanding the world through thermodynamics, the special theory of relativity, cybernetics, linearity, succession, and teleology continue to dominate our temporal understanding of history. The idea of empty and homogeneous time and its divisions into past, present, and future, still operate in such a way in history in general and in the history of the present time in particular that, for some, it has become a mythical thought (Blumenberg 1985; Hamann 2016; Simon and Tamm 2023). To quote Serres (1995), historians would behave like flat-earthers by ignoring scientific advances and not incorporating them into their way of understanding the world.

In *The Fabric of Historical Time* (2023), Zoltan Simon and Marek Tamm provide a comprehensive synthesis of the numerous temporal configurations that have been proposed as alternatives to the notion of absolute and linear time in history in recent decades. The redefinition of the past–present relationship through paradigms such as "presence," the recognition of indigenous temporalities, the challenges posed by both techno-scientific futures and the impact of climate change and the Anthropocene are examples of the existence of alternative temporalities and historicities that develop at different paces and have already solidified within the field of "times studies." The authors acknowledge an increasingly strong consensus that absolute and homogeneous time is just one element within a complex network of multiple temporal relations. They refer to this network of temporal relations as "the fabric of historical time."

In *History without Chronology* (2019), Stefen Tanaka also contributes to the diagnosis of the mythical nature of absolute and homogeneous time that has dominated historical studies. Linearity has ignored the multiple times that coexist and operate within events, failing to consider them as the means in which events develop and occur. According to Tanaka, chronology was the tool that absolute and linear time used to homogenize and domesticate, in the name of supposed objectivity and neutrality, the relativity, precariousness, and contextuality of the multiple temporal interactions of events. The world is not the orderly result of a universal system, as was the goal of the Enlightenment. The imposition of chronological metrics regulated the temporal dimension, concealing our limitations and the inevitable uncertainty we face when accepting the plurality and heterogeneity of temporalities that intersect our lives. In the same line of criticism of chronology, we find *Heterocronías: Estudios sobre a multiplicidade dos tempos históricos* (*Heterochronies: Studies on the Multiplicity of Historical Times*), a compilation of works by European and Brazilian authors edited by Marlon Salomon and published in 2018. This compilation also attempts to explore, from various perspectives, the multiplicity of temporalities and the inadequacy of the "arrow of time" as an assumption that once underpinned the field of history.

These three books are excellent examples of the critique numerous authors have carried out against the hegemonic position of absolute time in history today, advocating for a relational perspective on the multiplicity of temporalities. Taking into consideration Lorenz's (2021) warning about the need to take the temporal plurality seriously without enclosing it within another "time container," Simon and Tamm (2023) assert that all these temporalities "coexist in a network of constant change, with relational arrangements of complex interactions" (p. 55).

However, if we survey the entire body of literature that, from the onset of the "memory boom" to anthropological and postcolonial studies, as well as the consideration of the Anthropocene, has compelled historians to reassess their temporal assumptions, the concept of the present is rarely, if ever, clearly defined. Even in the field of the history of the present time, where the present is the central focus, it is often delineated through the lens of chronology. Even when attempting a phenomenological approach, such as exploring "lived time" or "generational time," the underlying presumption of linearity persists. In effect, either a sequential progression continues to be assumed, as exemplified by the previously mentioned Hartog citation, or the present is indirectly referred to as the "point" of "intersection," "articulation," or "coexistence" among various temporalities, whether they be psychological, political, social, cultural, geological, biological, or digital. Metaphors of "coexistence" and "articulation" of multiple temporalities are commonly used to describe the present, yet the precise nature of their coexistence and how they are interconnected and related, in essence, what defines the present, remains unexplained.

In 1769, in his work *Le Rêve de d'Alembert*, Denis Diderot employs the metaphor of the clavichord, likening it to a network of interconnected fibers, to convey that physiological reality is far more intricate than the dichotomy proposed by Descartes, which separated the mind from the body. When a string on the clavichord is struck, it resonates, much like a fiber woven within a network, eliciting another sensation or sound in an adjacent fiber or string. Diderot's spatial analogy of a network offers him the advantage of not constraining thought within a one-way, binary structure. Here, not only can two thoughts coexist simultaneously, but this network framework also allows him to conceive the concurrent unfolding of a multitude of mental events. The comparison of the mind to a network of fibers assists Diderot in envisioning a more intricate model of relationships between thoughts. This model encompasses not just inductive or deductive relationships but also those of harmony, dissonance, similarity, difference, and various other nuances. According to Diderot, mental reality is more closely aligned with a network of fibers than with a discrete substance isolated from the body (Anderson 1990).

This metaphor of the network was also adopted in the 1960s by the biologist Conrad Waddington. Alongside other visual concepts, it aided in grasping the intricacy of the epigenetic landscape, which, in his perspective, extended beyond the phenomena described by conventional biology (Waddington 1966). Despite its adaptability, this notion gained prominence as it transcended the confines of biology and found its way into the formulation of actor-network theory (ANT) during the 1980s, thanks to the contributions of scholars like Bruno Latour, Michel Callon, John Law, and others. The idea of a network or web underscores the significance of relationships and activities over static entities, substances, events, or agents. It is predominantly applied in the realm of sociology, where it emphasizes the advantages of accentuating the social as intricate networks of relationships. Giles Deleuze and Felix Guattari also express this idea of network using the metaphor of the rhizome. This metaphor adheres to principles of connection and heterogeneity: "any point of a rhizome can be connected to anything other, and must be" (Deleuze and Guattari 1987, p. 7); to principles of multiplicities: "it is only when the multiple is effectively treated as a substantive, 'multiplicity,' that it ceases to have any relation to the One as subject or object, natural or spiritual reality, image and world. Multiplicities are rhizomatic, and expose arborescent pseudomultiplicities for what they are" (p. 8); to principles of reallocation of ruptures: "against the oversignifying breaks separating structures or cutting across a single structure. A rhizome may be broken, shattered at a given spot, but it will start up again on one of its old lines, or on new lines" (p. 9); among others.

Vincent Descombes, in 1999, published "Qu´est-ce qu´etre contemporaine?" ("What Does It Mean to Be Contemporary?"), a pioneering work in attempting to define the present in history, abandoning all linear and chronological presuppositions. For Descombes, the adjective "contemporary" should not be applied to individuals. Individuals are contemporaneous in a derived sense; they are contemporaneous because their activities are contemporaneous. Similar to Diderot and Waddington in the biological realm and ANT in the social realm, Descombes prioritizes relationships and activities to account for the present. Describing what is contemporary doesn't require a list of names but rather "a state of places, a state of ongoing processes, and, above all, a state of the interaction of these processes and how they combine or counteract each other" (p. 29). Chronology doesn't define anything beyond an indifferent contemporaneity. The historical present, or what Descombes calls historical actuality, "consists of the historical interaction of ongoing processes, a source of interference." The contemporary appears as a set of activities that, because they occur simultaneously, either counteract or reinforce one another. Descombes's article largely went unnoticed in the field of history.

Bruno Latour's analysis of ANT as formulated by Michel Callon in 1986 supports an ontology expressed in terms of a network rather than substances or events. In this theory, the word "network" doesn't carry the technical sense associated with computer networks, nor does it have the social sense it acquires in sociology. In the computer domain, the word "network" is linked to a final and stable state of densely connected nodes found in computational networks. In sociology, although the term "network" aims to emphasize social relationships, these are often reduced to the actions of individual human actors. For Latour, both of these senses are limiting. He intends to give it the depth that Diderot attributed to the word "réseau" when he coined it, explicitly to avoid Descartes' mind–body dichotomy. From the outset, this notion has a strong ontological component. "To put it simply, ANT is a change of metaphors for describing essences; instead of surfaces, we have filaments (or rhizomes, as Deleuze would say)" (Latour 1996, p. 370).

Actor-network theory is, more precisely, a change in topology, and Latour confines it to the spatial realm. However, I want to extend it to the plurality of time and account for the present from a relational perspective. For Latour, instead of thinking in terms of surfaces or spheres, one should consider nodes with many connections. Actor-network theory allows us to use metaphors like capillaries, nerves, threads, and fibers that interconnect and provide a better description of contemporary societies than metaphors of layers, levels, territories, spheres, categories, structures, or systems. The strength of metaphors lies not in "concentration, purity, and unity but in the dissemination, heterogeneity, and careful weaving of weak threads" (Latour 1996, p. 370). Instead of starting with general laws, whether natural or social, to analyze local contingencies, ANT begins with these incomparable and irreducible localizations that sometimes end up temporarily in commensurable connections. Universality and order are not the rule but the exceptions.

Latour outlines three simple properties of networks, which are modified when an actor is introduced. These basic properties, common to all networks, allow us to reconsider, from a different perspective, the challenges posed to history by a linear, chronological, and universal temporal ontology.

The first property Latour mentions is the opposition of distant/close, which allows us to break free from the "tyranny of distance": "Elements which are close when disconnected may be infinitely remote when their connections are analyzed conversely, elements which would appear as infinitely distant may be close when their connections are brought back into the picture" (p. 371). Latour is referring to space. One of his examples is that a person can be one meter away from another but be more connected (closer) to another person who is 6,000 kilometers away (such as their mother). Although Latour is thinking about geographical categories that use measurements, triangulations, and mapping systems to determine the "distance" or "closeness" of objects, we can also extend this concept to history. The famous "temporal distance," measured in years and centuries, which was required for the past to be considered "historical," is a result of the linear chronology that operates as an ontological temporal principle, with its "epistemic" counterpart being the principle of "objectivity." The historical past "moves away" behind a present that is conceived as a point on the timeline. However, if we think in terms of networks and nodes, events considered "remote" from the standpoint of chronology can be "close" if we consider the relationships we establish in the present. The past events considered "distant," which are evoked, for example, by statues like those of Christopher Columbus, Borba Gato, Pedro de Valdivia, or General Roca and have been vandalized in racialized and colonized Latin American countries (Avelar 2022), belong to our present because of the networks we create with them, and they affect us more than other events that are "closer" in time from the perspective of linear chronology, such as the 2018 legislative elections in Iceland. The distant/close pair, reformulated in terms of a temporal network, allows us to navigate the difficulties in defining the "recent past." The "recent" or "distant" nature of a past event is not measured in years but in terms of the meaningful relationships that affect us. Understanding the past as "capillaries" in a temporal network that infiltrates and interweaves rather than as "distant" from the present point on a chronological line also leads us to reconsider the principle of "objectivity." The historian is an integral part of the network, not external to it, which means that "objectivity cannot exist" because both the "facts" and the scholar who gives them meaning are part of the fabric of relationships (Tanaka 2019, p. 102). The present has no epistemic privilege over the past; it does not constitute an "observatory" of the past. "When we ignore the 'temporal distance' (and presumption of advancement) enforced by dates, we can see a different 'reality.' For example, we open up the possibility of connections between our current states and pasts, what some are calling 'deep time'" (p. 11).

The second property is the small scale/large scale opposition. According to Latour, the notion of a network allows us to dissolve this distinction from the micro to the macro, which permeates all of social theory and, we can add, history. "The whole metaphor of scales going from the individual to the nation state, through family, extended kin, groups, institutions etc. is replaced by a metaphor of connections" (Latour 1996, p. 371). A network is never larger than another; it is simply more or less connected. With this metaphor, we avoid problems that arise when we think that, for example, an element belonging to the micro scale has a different nature and therefore must be studied differently from another element belonging to a larger scale. This is what, for Latour, creates the "axiological myth of a top and a bottom of society." This problem, which appears in social theory that presupposes a substantialist ontology, is replicated in most analyses of multiple temporalities in the field of history. It's the mismatch that would occur, for example, between the short-term time of political events and the long-term geographical time of Braudel, or the incommensurability Chakrabarty expressed between the scale of human time and the scale of geological time in the Anthropocene (Retz 2022). Instead of thinking in terms of strata, layers, and scales of different phenomena that oppose, overlap, and express incompatibilities of magnitudes, or proposing solutions for "synchronization" between multiple temporalities and different historiographical regimes, we should think of the metaphor of the temporal network that allows us to pay attention to the quantity of connections and relationships that occur, resulting in phenomena. The notion of a network applied to time dispenses with the category of scales that divides "things" or "events" into "larger" and "smaller" and instead focuses on the degree of connectivity that is established. "Things" or "events" are the result of relationships. Instead of the commonly expressed temporal idea that phenomena of different temporalities "coexist" in the same present, we should emphasize the relationships established between those that we assume operate on different scales.

The third characteristic Latour recognizes in the metaphor of the network is the inside/outside pair. Always keeping the spatial dimension in mind, Latour asserts that the notion of a network allows us to break free from the third dimension: from an inside and an outside separated by a boundary. "Literally, a network has no outside" (Latour 1996, p. 372). A network is a positive notion that does not need negativity to be understood. If we think about this in the context of the temporality of history, this characteristic can be translated into the foundational opposition in history and the social sciences between the human, the "inside" of history, and nature, the "outside" of history and the social sciences. History as an academic discipline, like the rest of the social sciences established during the nineteenth century, was founded on the distinction between natural processes and social and human processes. The classical notion of history, which still prevails, is that the discipline focuses on "human affairs," especially political and economic ones. This distinction is expressed clearly by Collingwood in 1946, who places nature outside the boundaries of history, which becomes the "background of history." For Collingwood, nature does not have history in the sense that humans can have it. However, conceiving of humans, from the perspective of the Anthropocene, as geophysical agents completely changes the conception of the nature/humanity dichotomy. It is no longer a matter of thinking that humans and nature influence each other recip- rocally, but rather that they are part of the same spatiotemporal network whose activities interconnect beyond intentional agency. On the other hand, the meta- phor of the network without an "outside" would help redefine the politics of time as normative decisions. Indeed, without an "outside," the notion of "peoples without history" or "backward cultures," expressions coined under the metaphor of "pushing back" in the timeline, makes no sense. The mere performa- tive act of expulsion or denial only serves to highlight the presence of the connec- tion and therefore enables resistance to be initiated. What does not enter into a relationship, even if it is through negative means, does not belong to the network.

As for the notion of an "actor," Latour points out that it has been subject to the same misunderstandings because it always refers, in the social and human sciences, to the intentional behavior of human actors. In ANT, on the contrary, Latour prefers the term "actant" to refer to anything that acts or possesses agency, which is not restricted to humans and includes nonhumans and nonindividual entities. An actant "implies no motivation of individual human actors, nor humans in general. An actant can be, literally, anything as long as it is a source of action. Although this point has been clarified time and time again, anthropocentrism and sociocentrism remain strong in the social sciences" (Latour 1996, p. 373). In this sense, we should avoid not only anthropocentrism but also what I call "anthropochronisms" concerning history. The concept of anthropochronism encompasses all expressions and categories used in the context of debates about historical time that assume "the human" as the agent of history. Categories such as presentism, presence, memory, regimes of historicity, chronopolitics, politics of time, and so forth ultimately constitute forms of anthropochronism. Despite the significant distinctions that may exist among them, all these concepts share one assumption: they refer to historical times of exclusively human worlds. Anthropochronisms belong to a tradition that considers the only inhabitants of the historical present and the "others" – whether they belong to the present, the past, or the future and are constituted by exclusion – to be us, humans. The fire and the fields scorched by the flames in Canberra, Australia, which Dipesh Chakrabarty observed in 2003 from a plane, are all actants whose relationships resulted, among other things, in "The Climate of History: Four Theses," published in 2009 in *Critical Inquiry*.

As mentioned earlier, the original sense of "cum tempus" – contemporary – was "living together" or "sharing the same time," meaning that the present was determined by those who shared activities. This relational way of defining the present was forgotten after absolute, linear, and chronological time became hegemonic. However, even though the memory boom, the "discovery" of "other" cultural temporalities, the deep time of the Anthropocene, among other issues, exposed its ontological assumptions and epistemological inconveniences, in most cases, what the present is has been completely overlooked through metaphors such as articulation or coexistence between pasts and futures or between multiple temporalities or overlapping times. And as Lorenz points out, although

> most thinkers have in common the fact that they reject the modernist idea that time is discrete, linear, unidirectional, and irreversible ... nevertheless, old habits usually die hard ... and many of those arguing for a plurality of times have not done so consistently and still have elements of that modernist idea, especially the idea of a uniform "container time" that functions as a 'container for all times. (Lorenz 2021)

I fully agree with Lorenz's critique, and I argue that the original notion of *cum tempus* associated with the concept of a network that we have been developing allows us to account for a present that does not fall into the "pitfall" of a "container for times."

In the original sense of contemporaneous, the metaphor of the network was implicitly present: those connected by filaments and networks of activities "lived together." However, we must broaden its scope, which originally had a human-centered focus. Now, "living together" refers to "actants" rather than just intentional human agents. This allows us to integrate nonhuman times that are interconnected. So, what is the present, or, even better, how can we determine the present? I understand the present as a temporal community, a community determined by those who "live together." This temporal community results from the interconnected activities of actants. In this sense, the notion of an "actant," following Latour, not only opens us up to nonhuman agents and events but also helps us understand history itself and the past as actants. They are "filters that people use to understand situations; they become constitutive conditions for every interaction. Events are interpreted (and altered) many times – by witnesses, historians, and readers" (Tanaka 2019, p. 153). By interpreting the notion of living together in terms of a network of actants, we move away from its original anthropocentric component and make a shift toward a relational temporal metaphor.

Tanaka, in an attempt to illustrate what it would mean to account for a time centered on activities in history, provides an example from Herodotus's *Historia*, a time when the concept of linear and homogeneous time did not exist. Herodotus relates the chronologies of Athens and Persia when the Persians invaded Athens: "Kalíades was the archon of Athens in the sixth year after the death of Darius, when Xerxes went to Greece" (Tanaka 2019, p. 71). We, in the language of linear and chronological time, translate this information into a discrete event: "The Persians invaded Athens in 480 BC." As we can see, translating event markers into dates completely transforms the understanding of events and their relationships. In a very different field, that of audiovisual media, Marsha Kinder refuses to date her ethnographic notes because she believes this form of dating implies objectification and separation from the subject. If we shift our focus from things to activities and relationships, it becomes more possible for our units of analysis to be based on "communities of practice," as Jean Lave and Etienne Wegner have termed them. Tim Ingold (1993) refers to this way of organizing the world as a "landscape of tasks," where action and interaction construct what he calls a "landscape." It is a landscape of connections and interrelationships, not a series of discrete events that occur in succession.

In summary, we began this work by trying to distinguish four senses of "contemporary." The first of them referred to the origin of the word, which derives from *cum tempus* and meant "sharing the same time." "Contemporary" was an adjective that related events and activities happening at the same time and appeared in France in 1475. This sense of "contemporary" should not be confused with that of "coetaneous," which indicates chronological synchronization. The original meaning aimed to point out that those who shared or were related through activities during medieval Europe perceived themselves as sharing the same present. In this way, many presents could be conceived as existing simultaneously. This scope of the term "contemporary" is lost when, during the last third of the eighteenth century and throughout the nineteenth century, the adjective "contemporary" began to designate the present as an epochal experience of time. This new experience or perception of the present distinguishes it very strongly from the past and the future. Taine, in nineteenth-century France, suggested that the French Revolution had introduced an insurmountable barrier between the (feudal) past and the new present. He called it "contemporary" to distinguish it from any previous present.

As the nineteenth century ends, another sense of "contemporary" emerges: "contemporary" as a period – that is, as a result of historiographical operation. "Contemporary" begins to mean, mainly in France, Germany, Spain, and Latin America, the period of time that encompasses the nineteenth century, which becomes the object of study in these countries as "contemporary history." But another transformation also occurs; "contemporary" begins to be equated with the present. For many historians, especially from the Anglo-Saxon tradition, "contemporary" and "present" were considered synonymous. "Contemporary" is understood as "historian's own life," "current times," or "the time we are passing through," implying that the present moves together with the historian on the timeline. Alongside this shifting of meanings, another problem arises: if "contemporary" is equal to "present," when does the "present" begin? According to different traditions and, fundamentally, considering disruptive national or epochal events, historians compete for different "beginnings" of the present or the contemporary period.

Also, during the 1980s, history felt the impact of the "memory boom." While discussions about the recent past and traumatic memories, mainly from wars, genocides, and military dictatorships, took place in the public sphere, this effervescence forced historians to review their ontological and epistemological assumptions, especially regarding temporal distance and its correlate of objectivity. In 1984, F. Bédarida coined the term "history of the present time" to describe the focus of the institute created by the CNRS in 1978. Bédarida preferred this name to differentiate it from the contemporary French present of the nineteenth century. Many other names are proposed: "histoire immédiate" in French; "contemporary history," "modern history," or even "instant history" in English; "Zeitgeschichte," "neuere," or "neueste Geschichte" in German; "historia vivida" or "pasado vivo" in Spanish; "tempo presente" in Portuguese, "pasado reciente" in Latin America. Along with the diversity of names, controversies about their "beginnings" also begin – that is, when does the present of the history of the present time begin? Currently, this subdiscipline has had different fates according to different contexts. While in Europe, for example, it is currently heavily criticized for being centered on the nation-state and political and/or traumatic events, in Latin America, it has an unusual momentum, extending its focus not only to issues of past dictatorships but also to indigenous peoples, Afro-descendants, and the Anthropocene. However, if we review all the discussions that have taken place regarding the different senses of the word "contemporary," the disparity of "beginnings," or the disputes over the names the history of the present time has received, we realize that the unquestioned assumption operating at the base is that of a linear, chronological, homogeneous, universal time external to events.

In the last part of the work, and following L. Descombes, L. Hölscher, B. Latour, D. J. Wilcox, and S. Tanaka, I argued in favor of a relational conception of time that allows us to overcome the problems mentioned earlier. I resumed the original sense of *cum tempus*, which referred to the present as the result of the relationships and activities of the men of the Middle Ages, and using mainly B. Latour's notion of the network, I tried to account for a relational present that is not anthropocentric. To conclude, neither Elon Musk's tweet, nor Lula's election, nor the 8 billion inhabitants are discrete events that "occur" "in" time. Neither Twitter's "accelerated" time, nor Lula's "short" time, nor the supposedly vast scale of the Anthropocene imply different, opposing, or incomparable strata. Therefore, conceiving the present as a temporal community of actants, and "living together" as the current concurrence of processes and activities, allows us to redefine historical time. The historical past is not the other of the present, something that has happened at an earlier time, nor is the future a period "after" the present. If we understand them in this way, we would be "traversing" only one of the "filaments" of time that make up the temporal community of those who "live together." This filament is the one that leads us to "time" and orders the world into successive events or "blocks" and periods of a single linear time. However, this is just one of the many threads interwoven in the present, which now appears as the contingent product of relationships that traverse temporal processes. We do not live immersed in events that happen without any connection, whether it's an earthquake, a plane crash, or a pandemic. We realize the existence of multiple times precisely because our activities collapse, relate to, integrate with, or repel the activities of "others." The challenge is to understand the world as the result of relationships that have a high degree of uncertainty, rather than as a more or less disconnected and catastrophic set of events. Indeterminacy, contingency, and complexity are the norm, not the exception, in this temporal community we all share. The past is not a distant or dead realm accessed by historians through archives. Instead, historians are themselves an integral part of that past, shaped by the relationships they forge with it. To truly grasp the notions of "historical pasts" and "historical futures," we must look within the interconnected unity of this community comprising current processes and activities. It is within this dynamic context that the strength of history lies, in transforming its tools to comprehend the sources of ambiguity and complexity within our present temporal community.

References

Agamben, G. (2009). What is the contemporary? In A. Groom, ed., *Time*. London: MIT Press, pp. 82–89.

Agulhon, M. (1981). *Marianne into Battle: Republican Imagery and Symbolism in France, 1789–1880*. Translated by J. Lloyd. Cambridge: Cambridge University Press.

Alaimo, S. (2016). *Exposed: Environmental Politics and Pleasures in Posthuman Times*. Minneapolis: University of Minnesota Press.

Alonso, L. (2010). Definiciones y tensiones en la formación de una Historiografía sobre el pasado reciente en el campo académico argentino. In J. A. Bresciano, ed., *El tiempo presente como campo historiográfico: Ensayos teóricos y estudios de casos*. Montevideo: Ediciones Cruz del Sur, pp. 41–64.

Altamira y Crevea, R. (1904). *Cuestiones modernas de historia*. Madrid: Daniel Jorro.

Alted, A. (1994). *Cómo hacer la historia contemporánea hoy: Conceptos, métodos y fuentes, curso 1994–95*. Madrid: Universidad Nacional de Educación a Distancia.

Anderson, W. (1990). *Diderot's Dream*. Baltimore, MD: Johns Hopkins University Press.

Araneda, D. M. (2016). La historia reciente en Chile: Un balance desde la nueva historia política. *Historia 396*, 6(1), 111–139.

Aravena, P. (2009). *Memorialismo, historiografía y política: El consumo del pasado en una época sin historia*. Concepción: Escaparate.

Aravena, P. (2014). Patrimonio, historiografía y memoria social: Presentismo radical y abdicación de la operación histórica. *Diálogo Andino*, 45, 77–84.

Aravena, P. (2022). *La inactualidad de Bolívar: Anacronismo, mito y conciencia histórica*. Valparaiso: RiL editores.

Aróstegui, J. (2004). *La historia vivida: Sobre la historia del presente*. Madrid: Alianza Editorial.

Ash, T. G. (1999). *History of the Present: Essays, Sketches and Despatches from Europe in the 1990s*. London: Knopf Doubleday.

Assis, A. A. (2023). *Plural Pasts: Historiography between Events and Structures*. Cambridge: Cambridge University Press.

Avelar, A. (2022). Por que a derrubada de estátuas não deveria incomodar os historiadores? Tempo, anacronismo e disputas pelo passado. *ArtCultura Uberlândia*, 24(44), 134–156.

Avelar, A., and Pereira, M. (2018). Ethics, present time and memory in Brazilian journals of history 1981–2014. *Historein*, 17(1). https://doi.org/10.12681/historein.8582.

Baram, A. (1991). *Culture, History and Ideology in the Formation of Ba'thist Iraq, 1968–80*. New York: St. Martin's Press.

Barraclough, G. (1964). *An Introduction to Contemporary History*. New York: Basic Books.

Barthes, R. (2003). *Cómo vivir juntos: Simulaciones novelescas de algunos espacios cotidianos (notas de los cursos en el Collège de France 1976–1977)*. Buenos Aires: Siglo XXI.

Barthes, R. (2009). What is the contemporary? In D. Kishik and S. Pedatella, eds., *What Is an Apparatus? And Other Essays*. Stanford, CA: Stanford University Press, pp. 39–54.

Bayle, P. (1820). *Dictionnaire Historique et Critique*. Paris: Desoer Libraire.

Beck, U. (1992). *Risk Society: Toward a New Modernity*. London: Sage.

Bédarida, F. (1998). Definición, método y práctica de la historia del tiempo presente. *Cuadernos de Historia Contemporánea*, 20, 19.

Bédarida, F. (2001). Le temps présent et l'historiographie contemporaine. *Vingtième Siècle: Revue d'Histoire*, 1(69), 153–160.

Bevernage, B. (2012). *History, Memory, and State-Sponsored Violence: Time and Justice*. New York: Routledge.

Bevernage, B., and Lorenz, C. (2013). *Breaking Up Time: Negotiating the Borders between the Present, Past and Future*. Gottingen: Vandenhoeck & Ruprecht.

Blight, D. W. (2009). The memory boom: Why and why now. In P. Boyer and J. Wertsch, eds., *Memory in Mind and Culture*. Cambridge: Cambridge University Press, pp. 238–251.

Bloch, E. (1991[1932]). Early condition. In *Heritage of Our Times*. Translated by N. Plaice, edited by Polity Press. Oxford: British Library, pp. 97–103. Kindle edition.

Bloch, M. (1952). *Apologie Pour l'Histoire ou Métier d'Historien (1949)*. París: Librairie Armand Colin.

Blumenberg, H. (1985). *Work on Myth*. Translated by R. M. Wallace. Cambridge, MA: MIT Press.

Bodnar, J. (1992). *Remaking America: Public Memory, Commemoration and Patriotism in the Twentieth Century*. Princeton, NJ: Princeton University Press.

Bohoslavsky, E., Franco, M., Lvovich, D. et al. (2010). *Problemas de la historia reciente del Cono Sur*. Buenos Aires: Prometeo.

Burges, J., and Elias, A. (2016). *Time: A Vocabulary of the Present*. New York: New York University Press.

Bustillo, J. C. (1993). *Historia del presente*. Salamanca: Ediciones de la Universidad Complutense.

Callón, M. (1986). Some elements of a sociology of translation: domestication of the scallops and the fishermen of St Brieux Bay. In J. Law, ed., *Power, Action and Belief: A New Sociology of Knowledge?* London: Routledee and Regan Paul, pp. 196–229.

Capdevila, L., and Langue, F. (2009). Invitation à une histoire comparée des temps présents. In L. Capdevila and F. Langue, eds., *Entre Mémoire Collective et Histoire Officielle*. Rennes: Presses Universitaires de Rennes, pp. 9–24.

Carr, D. (1986). *Time, Narrative and Knowledge*. Indianapolis: Indiana University Press.

Carr, E. H. (1983). *¿Qué es historia?* Barcelona: ARIEL, S. A.

Carson, R. (1962). *Silent Spring*. Boston, MA: Houghton Mifflin.

Caruth, C. (1996). *Unclaimed Experience: Trauma, Narrative, and History*. Baltimore, MD: Johns Hopkins University Press.

Cattaruzza, A. (2011). Las representaciones del pasado: Historia y memoria. *Boletín del Instituto de Historia Argentina y americana Dr. Emilio Ravignani*, 32(January–December), 155–164.

Cattaruzza, A. (2017). El pasado como problema político. *Anuario IEHS*, 32(2), 59–79.

Catterall, P. (1997). What (if anything) is distinctive about contemporary history? *Journal of Contemporary History*, 32(4), 441–452.

Certau, M. de (2007). *La escritura de la historia*. Mexico City: Universidad Iberoamericana.

Cezar, T. (2012). Escrita da história e tempo presente na historiografia brasileira. In F. Varella et al., eds., *Tempo presente e usos do passado*. Rio de Janeiro: Fundação Getulio Vargas.

Chakrabarty, D. (2000). *Provincializing Europe: Postcolonial Thought and Historical Diference*. Princeton, NJ: Princeton University Press.

Chakrabarty, D. (2004). Where is the now? *Critical Inquiry*, 30(2), 458–462.

Chakrabarty, D. (2009). The climate of history: Four theses. *Critical Inquiry*, 35(2), 197–222. https://doi.org/10.1086/596640.

Chakrabarty, D. (2015). *Lecture I: Climate Change As Epochal Consciousness. The Tanner Lectures in Human Values*. New Haven, CT: Yale University Press.

Chakrabarty, D. (2021). *The Climate of History in a Planetary Age*. Chicago, IL: University of Chicago Press.

Chateaubriand, F. R. (1848). *Mémoires d'Outre Tombe*. Paris: E. et V. Penaud Frères.

Christian, D., Bonneuil, N., Runia, E., et al. (1964). *History and Theory: The Next Fifty Years (Theme Issue 49, 2010) (History and Theory: Studies in the Philosophy of History)*. Middletown, CT: Wesleyan University.

Collingwood, R. G. (1994[1946]). *The Idea of History: With Lectures 1926–1928*. Oxford: Oxford University Press.

Crevea, A. Y., and Rafael Altamira (1904). *Cuestiones modernas de historia*. Madrid: Jorro.

Cuesta Bustillo, J. (1993). *Historia del presente*. Salamanca: Ediciones de la Universidad Complutense.

Daddow, O. (2004). Debating history today. *Rethinking History*, 8(1), 143–147.

Danto, A. (1985). *Narration and Knowledge: Including the Integral Text of Analytical Philosophy of History*. New York: Columbia University Press.

Déclaration de Naissance (1984). *Vingtième Siècle: Revue d'Histoire*. Paris: Sciences Po University Press.

Deleuze, G., and Guattari, F. (1987). A thousand plateaus: Capitalism and schizophrenia. Minneapolis: University of Minnesota Press

Derrida, J. (2004). Autoimmunity: Real and symbolic suicides. In G. Borradori, ed., *Philosophy in a Time of Terror: Dialogues with Jürgen Habermas and Jacques Derrida*. Chicago, IL: Chicago University Press, pp. 85–136.

Descombes, V. (1999). Qu'est-ce qu'être contemporain? *Le Genre humain*, 35, 21–32.

Diderot, D. (1975[1769]). *Le Rêve de d'Alembert*. In D. Diderot, ed., *Œuvres Complètes*. Paris: Hermann.

Diderot, D., and d'Alambert, J. (1751). Discourse Préliminaire. In *Encyclopédie, ou Dictionnaire raisonné des sciences, des arts et des métiers*, vol. 1, pp. I–xiv. https://fr.wikisource.org/wiki/L%E2%80%99Encyclop%C3%A9die/1re_%C3%A9dition/Discours_pr%C3%A9liminaire.

Diffenbaugh, N. S., Field, C. B., Appel, E. A., et al. (2020). The COVID-19 lockdowns: A window into the earth system. *Nature Reviews Earth & Environment*, 1(9), 470–481.

Droit, E., and Reichherzer, F. (2013). La fin de l'histoire du temps présent telle que nous l'avons connue: Plaidoyer franco-allemand pour l'abandon d'une singularité historiographique. *Vingtieme Siecle: Revue d'Histoire*, 118(2), 121–145.

Dutrénit, S., and Varela G. (2010). *Tramitando el pasado: Violaciones a los derechos humanos y agendas gubernamentales en casos de Latinoamérica*. Mexico City: Facultad Latinoamericana de Ciencias Sociales/Consejo Latinoamericano de Ciencias Sociales.

Elias, N. (1992). *Time: An Essay*. Oxford: Basil Blackwell.

Esthel, A. (2013). *Futurity: Contemporary Literature and the Quest of the Past.* Chicago, IL: University of Chicago Press.

Fabian, J. (1983). *Time and the Other: How Anthropology Makes Its Object.* New York: Columbia University Press.

Falcon, F. (2013). História e memória: Origens e desenvolvimiento do programa de pós-graduação em História da Universidade Federal Fluminense. *História da Historiografia*, 11, 15–32.

Felman, S., and Laub, D. (1992). *Testimony: Crisis of Witnessing in Literature, Psychoanalysis, and History.* New York: Routledge.

Ferreira, M. D. M. (2018). Notas iniciais sobre a história do tempo presente e a historiografia no Brasil. *Revista Tempo e Argumento*, 10(23), 80–108.

Foster, S. W. (1988). *The Past Is Another Country: Representation, Historical Consciousness, and Resistance in the Blue Ridge.* Los Angeles: University of California Press.

Franco, M. (2020). *Consideraciones sobre política e historiografía: El campo de la historia reciente en la Argentina.* Mexico City: Bonilla Artigas Editores.

Franco, M., and Levín, F. (2007). *Historia reciente: Perspectivas y desafíos para un campo en construcción.* Buenos Aires: Paidós.

Friedländer, S. (1992). *Probing the Limits of Representation*: *Nazism and the "Final Solution."* Cambridge, MA: Harvard University Press.

Gabriel, M. (1894). Victor Duruy. *Revue Internationale de l'Enseignement*, 28, 481–9.

Gadamer, H. G. (1989). *Truth and Method.* New York: Crossroad.

Garcia, P. (2003). Essor et enjeux de l'histoire du temps présent au CNRS. *La Revue Pour l'Histoire du CNRS* [En ligne], 9 | 2003, mis en ligne le 05 septembre 2007, consulté le 20 mai 2021. http://journals.openedition.org/histoire-cnrs/562. https://doi.org/10.4000/histoire-cnrs.562 (9).

Garcia, P. (2010). Histoire du temps présent. In C. Delacroix, F. Dosse, P. Garcia and N. Offenstadt, eds., *Historiographies: Concepts et débats.* Paris: Gallimard, pp. 282–294.

Garcia, P. (2018). L'histoire du temps présent: Une histoire comme les autres? *Mélanges de la Casa de Velázquez. Nouvelle Série* (48–2). https://doi.org/10.4000/mcv.8403.

Garmiño Muñoz, R. (2020). La historia vivida y el estudio de la violencia en México: Conflictos historiográficos y dilemas metodológicos. In E. Allier Montaño et al., eds., *En la Cresta de la Ola: Debates y definiciones en torno a la historia del tiempo presente.* Mexico City: Bonilla Artigas Editores, p. 490.

Groom, A. (2013). *Time.* London: MIT Press.

Grosfoguel, R. (2000). Developmentalism, modernity, and dependency theory in Latin America. *Nepantla: Views from South*, 1(2): 347–374.

Hacking, I. (1995). *Rewriting the Soul: Multiple Personality and the Sciences of Memory*. Princeton, NJ: Princeton University Press.

Hamann, B. (2016). How to chronologize with a hammer, Or, The myth of homogeneous, empty time.| *Journal of Ethnographic Theory*, 6(1), 261–329.

Harari, Y. N. (2014). *Sapiens: A Brief History of Humankind*. New York: Harper Collins.

Harari, Y. N. (2016). *Homo Deus: A Brief History of Tomorrow*. New York: Harper Collins.

Hartog, F. (2000). El historiador y el testigo. *Gradhiva*, 27, 1–14.

Hartog, F. (2003). *Régimes D'historicité: Présentisme et Expériences du Temps*. Paris: Le Seuil.

Hartog, F. (2015). *Regimes of Historicity: Presentism and Experiences of Time*. New York: Columbia University Press.

Henderson, G. B. (1941). A plea for the study of contemporary history. *History*, 26(101), 51–55.

Herodotus (1947). *Historiai*. Barcelona: Círculo Bibliófilo.

Hirsch, H. (1995). *Genocide and the Politics of Memory*. Chapel Hill: University of North Caroline Press.

Hölscher, L. (1999). *Die Entdeckung der Zukunft [The Discovery of the Future]*. Frankfurt: S. Fischer.

Hölscher, L. (2014). *El descubrimieto del futuro*. Madrid: Siglo XXI.

Huizinga, J. (1990). *Briefwisseling*. Edited by L. Hanssen, W. E. Krul, and A. van der Lem. Utrech: Veen. Quoted in Hollander, J., Paul, H., and Peters, R. (2011). Introduction: The metaphor of historical distance. *History and Theory*, Theme Issue 50, 2, 1–10.

Hutton, P. (1993). *History As an Art of Memory*. Lebanon, NH: University Press of New England.

Huyssen, A. (2007). *En busca del futuro perdido: Cultura y memoria en tiempos de globalización*. Buenos Aires: Fondo de Cultura Económica .

Iggers, G. (2005). *Historiography in the Twentieth Century: From Scientific Objectivity to the Postmodern Challenge*. Middletown, CT: Wesleyan University Press.

IHTP. (no date). L'institut d'Histoire du temps présent. www.ihtp.cnrs.fr/linsti tut-dhistoire-du-temps-present.

Ingold, T. (1993). The temporality of the landscape. *World Archaeology*, 25(2), 152–174.

International Meridian Conference. (1884). www.thegreenwichmeridian.org/ tgm/articles.php?article=10.

Kant, I. (2017). *Idea for a Universal History with a Cosmopolitan Purpose by Immanuel Kant*. Delphi Classics (Illustrated) ([edition unavailable]). Delphi Classics (Parts Edition). www.perlego.com/book/1655062/idea-for-a-univer sal-history-with-a-cosmopolitan-purpose-by-immanuel-kant-delphi-clas sics-illustrated-pdf (Original work published 2017).

Klein, K. L. (2000). On the emergence of memory in historical discourse. *Representations*, 69, 127–50. https://doi.org/10.2307/2902903.

Kleinberg, E. (2017). *Haunting History: For a Deconstructive Approach to the Past*. Stanford, CA: Stanford University Press.

Koselleck, R. (2004). *Future Pasts: On the Semantics of Historical Times*. Translated and with an introduction by Keith Tribe. New York: Columbia University Press.

LaCapra, D. (2001).*Writing History, Writing Trauma*. Baltimore, MD: Johns Hopkins University Press.

LaCapra, D. (2004). *History in Transit: Experience, Identity, Critical Theory*. Ithaca, NY: Cornell University Press.

Lagrou, P. (2003). Ou comment se constitue et se développe un nouveau champ disciplinaire. *La Revue Pour l'Histoire du CNRS*, 9. https://doi.org/10.4000/histoire-cnrs.561.

Landwehr, A. (2014). *Geburt der Gegenwart: Eine Geschichte der Zeit im 17 Jahrhundert [Birth of the Present: A History of Time in the Seventeenth Century]*. Frankfurt: S. Fischer.

Langmuir, G. (1990). *History, Religion, and Antisemitism*. Berkeley: University of California Press.

Latour, B. (1996). On actor-network theory: A few clarifications. *Soziale Welt*, 47(4), 369–381.

Latour, B. (2007). *Nunca fuimos modernos: Ensayos de antropología simétrica*. Buenos Aires: Siglo XXI Editores.

Lave, J., and Wenger, E. (1991). *Situated Learning: Legitimate Peripheral Participation*. Cambridge: Cambridge University Press.

Le Goff, J. (1980). Merchant's time and church's time in the Middle Ages. In *Time, Work, and Culture in the Middle Ages*. Translated by Arthur Goldhammer. Chicago, IL: University of Chicago Press, pp. 29–42.

Le Goff, J. (1992). *History and Memory*. Translated by S. Rendall and E. Claman. New York: Columbia University Press.

Le Goff, J. (2015). *Must We Divide History into Periods?* New York: Columbia University Press.

Li, L. Y. (2007). A few problems in the study of Chinese contemporary history. *Journal of Jiangsu University*, 2, 29–36.

Libera, A. de (2000). *La filosofía medieval*. Buenos Aires: Editorial Docencia.

Lorenz, C. (2010). Unstuck in time: Or the sudden presence of the past. In K. Tilmans, F. van Vree and J. Winter, eds., *Performing the Past: Memory, History, and Identity in Modern Europe*. Amsterdam: Amsterdam University Press, pp. 67–105.

Lorenz, C. (2014). It takes three to tango: History between the "practical" and the "Historical" past. *Storia della Storiografia*, 65(1), 29–46.

Lorenz, C. (2017). "The times they are a-changin": On time, space and periodization in history. In M. Carretero, S. Berger and M. Grever, eds., *Palgrave Handbook of Research in Historical Culture and Education*. London: Palgrave Macmillan, pp. 109–132.

Lorenz, C. (2021). Taking plural times seriously: Comments on Ethan Kleinberg's Koselleck lecture (Unpublished paper presented at the Institut für soziale Bewegungen, Bochum, December 14, 2021).

Lübbe, H. (1983). *Zeit-Verhältnisse: Zur Kulturphilosophie des Forstschritts*. Graz/Viena/Colonia: STyria.

Maier, C. S. (1993). A surfeit of memory? Reflections on history, melancholy and denial. *History and Memory*, 5(2), 136–152.

Mandelbaum, M. (1967). Historicism. In P. Edwards, ed., *The Encyclopedia of Philosophy*. New York: Macmillan.

Mandrini, R. (2007). La historiografía Argentina, los pueblos originarios y la incomodidad de los historiadores. *Quinto Sol*, 11, 19–38.

Marrou, H. I. (1954). *De la Connaissance Historique*. Paris: Le Seuil.

Maza, S. (2017). *Thinking about History*. Chicago, IL: University of Chicago Press.

Megill, A. (1998). History, memory, identity. *History of the Human Sciences*, 11(3), 37–62.

Mieroop, K. van de. (2016). The "age of commemoration" as a narrative construct: A critique of the discourse on the contemporary crisis of memory in France. *Rethinking History*, 20(2), 172–191.

Montaño, E. A. (2015). De historias y memorias sobre el pasado reciente en Uruguay: Treinta años de debates. *Caravelle*, 104, 133–150.

Montaño, E. A., Ortega, C. I. V., and Ovalle, C. V. (2020). *En la Creta de la Ola: Debates y definiciones en torno a la historia del tiempo presente*. Mexico City: Universidad Nacional Autónoma de México .

Morgan, S., Jenkins, K., and Munslow, A. (2007). *Manifestos for History*. New York: Routledge.

Mudrovcic, M. I. (2003). Alcances y límites de perspectivas psicoanalíticas en historia. *Revista de Filosofía DIÁNOIA*, 48(50), 111–127.

Mudrovcic, M. I. (2005). Algunas consideraciones epistemológicas para una "historia del presente." In M. I. Mudrovcic, ed., *Historia, narración y memoria: Debates actuales en la filosofía de la historia.* Madrid: Akal, pp. 120–132.

Mudrovcic, M. I. (2009). Representar pasados en conflicto. In M. I. Mudrovcic, ed., *Pasados en conflicto: Representación, mito y memoria.* Buenos Aires: Prometeo.

Mudrovcic, M. I. (2016). Historical narrative as a moral guide and the present as history as an ethical project. *História da Historiografía: International Journal of Theory and History,* 9(21), 10–24.

Mudrovcic, M. I. (2019). The politics of time, the politics of history: Who are my contemporaries? *Rethinking History,* 23(4), 456–473.

Mudrovcic, M. I. (2021). El presente suspendido y la experiencia del evento sin precedentes: A propósito de la pandemia del COVID-19. *Cuadernos de Historia (Santiago),* 55, 37–58. https://doi.org/10.4067/S0719-12432021000200037.

Nava, R. (2015). *Deconstruir el archivo: La historia, la huella y la ceniza.* Mexico City: Universidad Iberoamericana.

Nora, P. (1978). Présent. In J. Le Goff, R. Chartier, and J. Revel, eds., *La Nouvelle Histoire.* Paris: Retz, pp. 467–472.

Nora, P. (1988). Presente. In J. Le Goff, R. Chartier, and J. Revel, eds., *La nueva historia.* Bilbao: Mensajero, pp. 531–537.

Nora, P. (1989). Between memory and history: Les lieux de mémoire. *Representations,* 26, 7–24. https://doi.org/10.2307/2928520.

Nora, P. (1997). *Les Lieux de Mémoire.* Paris: Gallimard.

Osterhammel, J. (2006). Über die Periodisierung der neueren Geschichte [On the periodization of modern history]. *Berlin-Brandenburgische Akademie der Wissenschaften, Berichte und Abhandlungen,* 10, 45–64.

Osterhammel, J. (2014). *The Transformation of the World: A Global History of the Nineteenth Century.* Translated by P. Camiller. Princeton, NJ: Princeton University Press.

Pascal, P. (1963). *Oeuvres Completes.* Paris: Seuil.

Pereira, M. (2015). Nova direita? Guerras de memória em tempos de Comissão da Verdade (2012–2014). *Vária Historia,* 31(57), 863–902.

Peter, M., and Schröder, H. J. (1994). *Einführung in das Studium der Zeitgeschichte.* Paderborn: Schöningh.

Petryna, A. (2002). *Life Exposed: Biological Citizens after Chernobyl.* Princeton, NJ: Princeton University Press.

Phillips, M. S. (2013). *On Historical Distance.* New Haven, CT: Yale University Press.

Postone, M. (1993). *Time, Labour and Social Domination: A Reinterpretation of Marx's Critical Theory.* Cambridge: Cambridge University Press.

Preidt, R. (2020). Coronavirus isn't even "alive," but expert explains how it can harm. www.medicinenet.com/script/main/art.asp?articlekey=229387.

Readman, K. S. (2011). Contemporary history in Europe: From mastering national pasts to the future of writing the world. *Journal of Contemporary History*, 46(3), 506–530.

Retz, T. (2022). *Progress and the Scale of History*. Cambridge: Cambridge University Press.

Reynold, G. de. (1957). *La Formation de l'Europe*, vols. 1–8. Fribourg: LUF Librairie de l'Université Egloff/Plon.

Ricoeur, P. (1983–5). *Temps et Récit*. Paris: Seuil.

Ricoeur, P. (2014). *La mémoire, l'histoire, l'oubli*. Paris: Le Seuil.

Ritter, G. (1961). Scientific history, contemporary history, and political science. *History and Theory*, 1(3), 261–279.

Ritter, H. (1986). *Dictionary of Concepts in History*. New York: Greenwood Press.

Rothberg, M. (2009). *Multidirectional Memory: Remembering the Holocaust in the Age of Decolonization*. Stanford, CA: Stanford University Press.

Rothfels, H. (1953). Zeitgesschichte als aufgabe. *Vierteljahrshefte für Zeitgeschichte*, 1, 1–8.

Rousso, H. (2000). L'histoire du temps présent, vingt ans après. *Bulletin de l'IHTP*, 75, 23–40.

Rousso, H. (2012). *La Dernière Catastrophe: l'Histoire, le Présent et le Contemporain*. Paris: Éditions Gallimard. (English edition: *The Latest Catastrophe: History, the Present, the Contemporary*. Translated by J. M. Todd. Chicago, IL: University of Chicago Press, 2016).

Rousso, H. (2016). Coping with contemporariness. In L. N. Brozgal and S. Kippur, eds., *Being Contemporary: French Literature, Culture, and Politics Today*. Liverpool: Liverpool University Press, pp. 15–28.

Runia, E. (2007). Burying the dead, creating the past. *History and Theory*, 46(3), 313–325.

Runia, E. (2014) *Moved by the Past: Discontinuity and Historical Mutation*. New York: Columbia University Press.

Rüsen, J. (2007). Introduction. In J. Rüsen, ed., *Time and History: The Variety of Cultures*. New York: Bergahn Books, pp. 1–4.

Ruthven, K. K. (1992). *Beyond the Disciplines: The New Humanities*. Canberra: Australian Academy of the Humanities.

Salomon, M. (ed.). (2018). *Heterocronias: Estudos sobre as multiplicidades do tempo histórico*. Goiânia: Edições Ricochete.

Sánchez, J. A. S. (2004). *La historia vivida: Sobre la historia del presente*. Madrid: Alianza Editorial.

Sánchez, J. A. S. (2006). La contemporaneidad, época y categoría histórica. *Mélanges de la Casa de Velázquez*, 36(1), 107–130.

Savidan, P., and Mesure, S. (2006). *Dictionnaire des Sciences Humaines*. Paris: Presses Universitaires de France.

Schiffman, Z. S. (2011). *The Birth of the Past*. Baltimore, MD: Johns Hopkins University Press.

Schlesinger Jr., A. (1967). On the writing of contemporary history. *The Atlantic*, 69–74. www.theatlantic.com/magazine/archive/1967/03/on-the-writing-of-contemporary-history/305731. Quoted in Ritter, H. (1986). *Dictionary of Concepts in History*. New York: Greenwood Press, p. 66.

Serres, M. (1995). The birth of time. In *Genesis*. Translated by G. James and J. Nielson. Ann Arbor: University of Michigan Press, pp. 81–122.

Seton-Watson, R. W. (1929). A plea for the study of contemporary history. *History*, 14(53), 1–18.

Simon, Z. B. (2019). *History in Times of Unprecedented Change*. London: Bloomsbury Academic.

Simon, Z. B. (2020). *The Epochal Event: Transformation in the Entangled Human, Technological, and Natural Worlds*. Cham: Palgrave Macmillan.

Simon, Z. B. (2021). Domesticating the future through history. *Time & Society*. Special Issue: Temporal Comparisons, s/c, May, pp. 1–23.

Simon, Z. B., and Tamm, M. (2023). *The Fabric of Historical Time*. Elements in Historical Theory and Practice. Edited by Daniel Woolf. Cambridge: Cambridge University Press.

Soler, L. (2000). *Historiografía uruguaya contemporánea (1985–2000)*. Montevideo: Editorial Trilce.

Soulet, J. F. (1999). L'histoire immédiate en Europe Occidentale. *Cahiers d'Histoire Immédiate*, 16, pp. 44–60.

Steinmetz, W., Simon, Z., and Postoutenko, K. (2021). Temporal comparisons: Evaluating the world through historical time. *Time & Society*, 30(4), 447–461.

Taine, H. (1986)[1828–93]. *Les origines de la France contemporaine*. Paris: Bouquins.

Tanaka, S. (2019). *History without Chronology*. Ann Arbor, MI: Lever Press.

Urteneche, G. (2022). Historia, tiempo y testimonio: La construcción del otro en la historiografía del pasado reciente. Doctoral Thesis. University of Buenos Aires.

Van der Kolk. B. (1994). *The Body Keeps the Score: Memory and the Evolving Psychobiology of Post Traumatic Stress*. Harvard, MA: Harvard Medical School.

Varella, F. et al. (2012). *Tempo presente e usos do passado*. Rio de Janeiro: Fundação Getulio Vargas.

Voltaire, F.-M. A. (1954[1751]). *El Siglo de Luis XIV.* Translated by Nélida Orfila Reynal. Mexico City: Fondo de Cultura Económica.

Voltaire (1751). Le Pyrrhonisme de l'histoire. *Oeuvres Complètes.* https://fr.wikisource.org/wiki/Le_Pyrrhonisme_de_l%E2%80%99histoire/%C3%89dition_Garnier.

Voltaire (1756). Correspondence. *Oeuvres Complètes.* https://fr.wikisource.org/wiki/Correspondance_de_Voltaire/1756/Lettre_3279.

Voltaire (1877). Poème sur le désastre de Lisbonne. *Oeuvres Complètes.* https://fr.wikisource.org/wiki/Po%C3%A8me_sur_le_d%C3%A9sastre_de_Lisbonne/%C3%89dition_Garnier.

Voltaire (1964). Verdad. *Diccionario filosófico.* Buenos Aires: Editorial Araujo. T. III, pp. 347–348.

Waddington, C. H. (1966). *Principles of Developmental Differentation.* New York: Macmillan.

White, H. (1973). *Metahistory: The Historical Imagination in Nineteenth-Century Europe.* Baltimore, MD: Johns Hopkins Universty Press.

White, H. (1992). Historical emplotment and the problem of truth. In S. Friedländer, ed., *Probing the Limits of Representation: Nazism and the Final Solution.* Cambridge, MA: Harvard Univesity Press.

White, H. (2014). *The Practical Past.* Evanston, IL: Northwestern University Press.

Wiesel, E. (1985). Auschwitz no puede ser explicado ni visualizado (…) el Holocausto trasciende a la historia. In E. Wiesel, ed., *Against Silence: The Voice and Vision of Elie Wiesel.* New York: Irving Abrahamson, Holocaust Library, p. 158.

Wilcox, D. (1987). *The Measure of Times Past: Pre-Newtonian Chronologies and the Rhetoric of Relative Time.* Chicago, IL: University of Chicago Press.

Wilder, G. (2022). *Concrete Utopianism: The Politics of Temporality and Solidarity.* New York: Fordham University Press.

Winter, J. (2001). The generation of memory: Reflections on the "memory boom" in contemporary historical studies. *Canadian Military History,* 10(3), 57–66.

Winter, J. (2006). *Remembering War: The Great War between Memory and History in the Twentieth Century.* New Haven, CT: Yale University Press.

Woodward, L. (1966). The study of contemporary history. *Journal of Contemporary History,* 1(1), 1–13.

Woolf, D. (2021). Getting back to normal: On normativity in history and historiography. *History and Theory,* 60(3), 469–512.

Woolf, D. (2023). Historical periodization: An exploration and defense. In A. Mahler and C. Zwierlein, eds., *Zeiten bezeichnen Frühneuzeitliche*

Epochenbegriffe: Europäische Geschichte und globale Gegenwart Labelling Times The "Early Modern" – European Past and Global Now. Gottingen: Herzog August Bibliothek.

Wolfenbüttel Woolf, D. (2001). News, history and the construction of the present in early modern England. In B. Dooley and S. Baron, eds., *The Politics of Information in Early Modern Europe*. London: Routledge, pp. 80–118.

Yerushalmi, Y. (1982). *Zakhor: Jewish History and Jewish Memory*. Seattle: University of Washington Press.

Yerushalmi, Y. (1989). Reflexiones sobre el olvido. In Y. Yerushalmi, N. Loreaux, H. Mommsen, J. C. Milner, and G. Vattimo, eds., *Usos del olvido*. Buenos Aires: Nueva Edición, pp. 13–26.

Zubeldia, C. N. (2003). El regreso de la "verdadera" historia contemporánea. *RHA*, 1(1), 143–162.

Cambridge Elements ≡

Historical Theory and Practice

Daniel Woolf
Queen's University, Ontario

Daniel Woolf is Professor of History at Queen's University, where he served for ten years as Principal and Vice-Chancellor, and has held academic appointments at a number of Canadian universities. He is the author or editor of several books and articles on the history of historical thought and writing, and on early modern British intellectual history, including most recently *A Concise History of History* (CUP 2019). He is a Fellow of the Royal Historical Society, the Royal Society of Canada, and the Society of Antiquaries of London. He is married with 3 adult children.

About the Series
Cambridge Elements in Historical Theory and Practice is a series intended for a wide range of students, scholars, and others whose interests involve engagement with the past. Topics include the theoretical, ethical, and philosophical issues involved in doing history, the interconnections between history and other disciplines and questions of method, and the application of historical knowledge to contemporary global and social issues such as climate change, reconciliation and justice, heritage, and identity politics.

Cambridge Elements ≡

Historical Theory and Practice

Elements in the Series

A full series listing is available at: www.cambridge.org/EHTP

Printed in the United States
by Baker & Taylor Publisher Services